Performative Inter-Actions
in African Theatre 3

Performative Inter-Actions in African Theatre 3: Making Space, Rethinking Drama and Theatre in Africa

Edited by

Kene Igweonu and Osita Okagbue

Performative Inter-Actions in African Theatre 3:
Making Space, Rethinking Drama and Theatre in Africa,
Edited by Kene Igweonu and Osita Okagbue

This book first published 2013

Cambridge Scholars Publishing

12 Back Chapman Street, Newcastle upon Tyne, NE6 2XX, UK

British Library Cataloguing in Publication Data
A catalogue record for this book is available from the British Library

ISBN (10): 1-4438-5250-3, ISBN (13): 978-1-4438-5250-0

As a three volume set: ISBN (10): 1-4438-5611-8, ISBN (13): 978-1-4438-5611-9

DEDICATED TO
The African Theatre Association (AfTA) and its many committed
members around the world.

CONTENTS

LIST OF ILLUSTRATIONS

INTRODUCTION

PERFORMATIVE INTER-ACTIONS IN AFRICAN THEATRE

KENE IGWEONU AND OSITA OKAGBUE

Introduction

Theatre and performance have always existed in Africa as part of the cultural process and practice of what it means to be human. In effect, this means that theatre and performance have usually been perceived as one among a multitude of cultural practices that communities have, and engage in. Thus, theatrical performance as both a cultural practice and a process continues to contribute—like all the other cultural practices—to the well-being of community members and the societies in which they exist, and sometimes this contribution can take the form of cultural revision and/or social change. For us, this is the basis for the *famed* principle of functionality that is believed to underpin all forms of theatre and performance in Africa.

It is our view, and this is clearly borne out by analysis and study, that all traditions of theatre in Africa—from the various indigenous performances such as the masquerade theatre, ritual performances, musical theatre, and Theatre for Development, to the more contemporary forms such as the video films of Nollywood—are functional at their most basic level. In other words, each performance form engages in a dialectical relationship of mutual affect with their respective local socio-cultural contexts. Consequently, we take the view in this book that the notion of performativity serves as an enabling and encompassing framework under which all forms of theatrical practice in, and about, Africa can best be analysed and understood.

The last four decades have witnessed an unprecedented rise in African theatre and performance scholarship. Following on from the early 1980s, much of the debate surrounding whether indigenous African performances

—rituals and festivals—constitute drama and theatre was quickly displaced by the rise of performance studies, which provided a useful framework with which to theorise non-western forms and practices. Since then, there has been a rise in the number of Africanist scholars who are beginning to theorise and analyse African theatre and performance by drawing on a range of indigenous frames of references—most of which acknowledge and extend, but do not necessarily accede to dominant western discursive frameworks.

As a consequence, in putting this publication forward at this time, we seek to acknowledge the concept of performativity—in the way it has been theorised in western performance scholarship—but ultimately go on to explore its relevance for African theatre and performance. However, in doing this, we hope to move on from the debates around the term "performativity", to explore notions of *inter-actions* in African theatre and performance. We equally extend our examination to how African theatre practitioners work today, with an active (not passive) recognition of international theatre practices, while striving to create works that remain locally relevant and that are rooted in indigenous practices—thus successfully negotiating the global vs. local shifts in theatre practice.

African theatre and performance is functional. In other words, it is not just entertainment but is often geared towards fulfilling particular social or aesthetic functions—hence, it is performative at its core. By focusing on the many and varied inter-actions evident in African theatre and performance practice, the chapters in this book set out to examine how recent advances in global citizenship, technology, economics, and trans-/inter-cultural transactions and borrowings have impacted on theatre and performance in Africa. In doing this, we take our lead from the recent debate about the significant challenges facing African theatre and performance practice, and broaden the discussion to include the many ingenious solutions adopted to tackle them by exploring the notion of inter-actions from different perspectives, including contacts, dealings, and connections across cultures, discipline, and media.

Importantly, our focus also extends beyond the debates on hybridity to examine contemporary performance forms in, and about, Africa that are *comfortable* in that very active process of negotiating an African identity that is globally aware, and yet locally relevant. However, a first step in this task is to set out how we understand and articulate performativity, and how it might relate to our unfolding discussion of these inter-actions that are so pervasive in African theatre and performance practice today.

Performativity in Performance or the Performativity of Performance

To begin with, a few questions that will be addressed in this introduction include: How does performativity differ from performance? Is performativity a central quality of African performance? How does the notion of performativity help us to understand ideas of presentation and representation in performance? Does performativity help in the understanding and presentation of the Self and Other? Is performativity a key element in the perception of theatre as culture in action, or of performance as a cultural process? Finally, is performativity a performance that does not end?

Ever since J. L. Austin, in his linguistic lectures, introduced the concept of the performative utterance, the idea of performativity or performative acts entered the language of performance theory. This concept has since continued to exercise scholars because the distinction between performance and performativity has not always been clear. We do not look to resolve this debate in this introduction, but we intend to show—through the various readings of scholars, from Austin through to Lyotard (who sees performativity as efficiency), Derrida, Lacan, Butler, Schechner to Harris, and Brocker—that it is the idea of performativity within performance that affords it its transformative potential.

In his lectures and, latterly, in his seminal book, *How to Do Things with Words* (1962), Austin differentiates between two kinds of utterances. The first he calls "constative utterances"—these are utterances that merely describe or report on a state of affairs—and the second he calls "performatives"—these refer to utterances which in their enunciation do things, bring the things they describe into being, or even *are* the things they describe. As Andrew Parker and Eve Kosofsky Sedgwick assert in the introduction to their edited collection, *Performativity and Performance*, that in doing so Austin unwittingly initiated the process that has led to an "oblique intersection between performativity and the loose cluster of theatrical practices, relations, and traditions known as performance" (1995: 1). However, they also point out, and as we indicate above, how very "un-articulated" the cross-purpose appropriation of Austin's term has been for performance theory.

The key problem for performance theory is that this appropriation of Austin's term does sometimes lead to an indiscriminate interchanging of the two terms by scholars, leading at times to imprecision and uncertainty in the meaning of the term, and at other times to total confusion. As Geraldine Harris correctly argues in *Staging Feminisms: Performance and*

Performativity (1999), much of this confusion can be attributed to Judith Butler's use of drag to demonstrate the performativity of gender in her seminal study, *Gender Trouble* (1990). But Butler, it should be pointed out, has also been at pains in her later work, *Bodies that Matter* (1993), to make "it clear that performativity refers to a '*process,* a reiteration of a norm or set of norms' while performance 'is a bounded act'" (Harris, 1999: 72).

Butler's differentiation, notwithstanding, this confusion still persists as both terms do have so much in common—so much that binds them to each other. In this book, we see the difference between performance and performativity as being in many ways reflective of the difference between reality and make-believe, between the real and the mimetic, between the presentation of reality and representation of the real. One other key difference between performance and performativity, as both Butler and Harris point out, is that although both share in the quality of citationality and reiteration, it is in the nature of what is being cited that they differ. For instance, one may ask the question, what is cited or repeated in performance—and for what purpose—, and what is cited or repeated in performativity—and for what purpose. The fact that in performance the citation is foregrounded and acknowledged, while this is not always the case in performativity, is one useful way of marking the difference between the two terms.

Thus, while a performative act and a performance act are alike in many ways, performance always involves and implies an awareness or consciousness of performing on the part of the performer. Whereas, in a performative act the "performer" is not always conscious of the fact that they are performing—hence the reason that Butler's study was ground-breaking, as well as controversial, in its claims regarding the performance of gender in everyday life. This is perhaps what Harris, echoing Butler, means, when she observes, "performance foregrounds its quotation marks (citation) whereas performativity in real life strives to conceal its citationality" (1999: 76). In other words, in performance the conventions of theatre, such as the framing, as well as the contexts and the rules are clear and often foregrounded, whereas in performative contexts these are mostly absent or are not necessarily rendered operative.

Performance, for Austin, is "acting or mimetically re-creating the real", while "the performative effects real change. It constitutes reality". (Blocker, 1999: 26) Blocker thus argues that performativity makes an artwork more than just an object or a theatrical performance, because "it helps reinforce the claim that the work actually makes something happen" (1999: 26). Performativity, therefore, when understood in uncluttered

Austinian terms as "doing" rather than "describing" can be very useful in appreciating and analysing the functionality and other characteristic manifestations of theatre in Africa. In most instances, theatre in Africa does not attempt or claim to represent reality; rather it presents a form of reality. It acknowledges that the line between the reality on stage and the reality in everyday life—between the worlds inhabited by the characters on stage and the performers that embody them—is not always as clearly demarcated or separated in Africa as it is in some other cultures of the world.

Another way we can explore the notion of performativity in African theatre, is to draw on the discursive framework derived from Jacques Derrida's idea of a generalised iterability of speech acts, which—according to Richard Schechner—supposes that "...meaning cannot be permanently fixed: every utterance is a repetition—just as stage speech is the repetition of a script" (2002: 125). By this approach we move away from Austin's argument for the exclusion of theatrical speech from the discussion of performativity, based on his claim that speech uttered by an actor on stage is "infelicitous" and does not truly reflect the speaker's intention. In fact, Austin's position is akin to that held by John R. Searle who "separates 'normal real world talk' from 'parasitic forms of discourse such as fiction, play acting, etc'" (Schechner, 2002: 126), when he contends that "people constructed their realities largely by means of speech acts; and they communicated these realities to each other by means of speech acts" (Schechner, 2002: 126). However, by drawing on Derrida and evidence of the continued blurring of the boundaries between what is generally considered to be fiction and reality, Schechner remarks that:

> Searle and Austin took this position because they didn't recognise that art can be a model for rather than, or in addition to, being a mirror of or escape from life. (2002: 126)

In his attempt to rehabilitate Austin's original thesis, however, James Loxley cites Austin's argument "that speech actually has the power to *make* a world" (Jackson cited in Loxley, 2007: 2), and uses it to claim that:

> The creative connotation of this "making" have also drawn in theorists of literary language, and a possible relation to theatrical performance has stimulated the interest of thinkers on drama. (Loxley, 2007: 2)

In putting forward this re-reading of Austin, Loxley articulates what he terms the standard narrative of origins and subsequent development of performativity, by which he attempts to bridge the gap between Austin's views and those expounded by the likes of Derrida and Butler. Going further along these lines, Loxley argues that Derrida's radical deconstruction of the notion of performativity led to its wider application to "pressing issues in cultural politics" (2007: 3). He goes on to add that:

> Such illumination of the way we "act" our identities also had radical implications for how we might think about the relation between theatrical performance and the apparently real or serious world offstage, implications that performance theorists have themselves sought to spell out in recent years. (Loxley, 2007: 3)

In this sense, performativity points to a variety of topics, among them the construction of social reality including gender and race, the restored behaviour quality of performances, and the complex relationships of performance practice to performance theory (Schechner, 2002: 123).

By way of going back to definitions, we cite copiously from Henry Bial who describes performativity, on the one hand, as a term that is often:

> invoked by those who wish to describe a performance without the connotations of artifice or superficiality that accompany the word "theatrical". (2007: 175)

Bial also goes on to add that, "[O]n another level, the term 'performative' refers to a specific philosophical concept concerning the nature and potential of language" (Bial, 2007: 175), in which speech denotes action, and saying *it* means to do *it*, or as Schechner puts it:

> [I]n uttering certain sentences people perform acts. Promises, bets, curses, contracts, and judgements do not describe or represent actions: they are actions. (2002: 123)

Seen from this perspective, and by interrogating the relationship between *speech* and *action*, we contend that utterances in African theatre do not always constitute attempts to express or convey existing reality in everyday life, but work to construct new, and often parallel, realities. This idea is deeply rooted in indigenous performance practices, such as the *mmonwu* (masquerade) performance of the Igbo people of eastern Nigeria. In most of these performances the poetic utterances of the *mmonwu*—who is seen as an embodiment of both ancestral and extant traditions of the people—lay bare present realities as they exist within the society, while simultaneously weaving their poetic narrative around an alternative reality drawn from a parallel universe or a vision of the future for the community at large.

Discussing the performative use of speech or narrative in African theatre, and the role of the playwright in that process of constructing a new or alternative reality, Esiaba Irobi argues that:

> Speech, you see, is a performance. Utterance. Incantation. Invocation. Chant. Ululation. Prayer. Even breathing is a performance. (That is why sometimes we snore heavily in a play to indicate—in the context of our make-belief—that we are asleep). (Azuonye, 2003)

While this idea of using various forms of *speech* to create new realities constitutes an interesting concept, African authors often find it difficult to capture some of the nuances of their indigenous languages in English or other languages of colonisation. Consequently, Irobi goes on to add that:

> an important qualification or credential for being a poet is to have that self-destructive perfectionist streak that makes you want to panel beat language into a shape accurate and broad-shouldered enough to carry the full weight of your experiences. (Azuonye, 2003)

On the one hand, therefore, this idea of "panel beating" western languages to fit indigenous references describes an approach used by successful playwrights on the African continent to respond performatively to the challenge of writing in an imperial language. Consequently, African theatre can be described as being dynamic—often making subversive use of English or other imperial languages in ways that are evocative of the idea of "panel beating" in order to convey indigenous imageries through the performative utterances of their characters.

On the other hand, however, African playwrights from the diaspora do not create characters that deliberately set out to undermine western languages by "panel beating" them in the same way as their continental counterparts. Instead, the performative utterances of their characters are often seen in the way they articulate their *migrant* identities in the western societies they have come to consider as *home*. Their characters speak in the same way as their non-African counterparts, but their utterances are often laden with deep political symbolisms and meanings that do not go unnoticed to the *Other* characters. In fact, their performative utterances are underpinned by a glaring realisation that their social condition is largely informed by their racial identity. Consequently, characters created by African diasporic playwrights often make performative utterances that position them firmly in the location in which they find themselves.

A good example of this can be found in the works of Dipo Agboluaje, who is famous for writing plays that satirise contestations of cultural identity in British society. His plays are inspired by both his Nigerian and British heritage, and strive to convey the experiences of the Nigerian diaspora living in Britain as "distinct in its finer details" from that of other black peoples living in Britain. Explaining this in a 2008 interview with Belinda Otas, he argues:

> Understanding the minutiae of life is what I try to do. I'm not one for emphasising the liberal assumption that we are all the same and that my job is then to go on and prove it. That breeds smug theatre, a theatre of recognition, preaching to the converted. There's no challenge in that. (Otas, 2008)

Through his plays, Agboluaje goes beyond posing a challenge to what it means to be a black person living in a "so called" multi-cultural British society, to raise questions about what it means to be British and Nigerian at the same time. In the same interview with Otas, Agboluaje explains:

> My voice has been created by two societies: Nigeria and Britain. For me that is an inescapable fact whatever politics of writing I might claim. As people of the Diaspora we inhabit diverse worlds: home communities back home, *home* communities within the host nation and relationships with other Diaspora communities. We respond to the politics of the society we are in. (Otas, 2003)

It is the complex nature of such a relationship, articulated in Agboluaje's plays, that is also echoed in different ways by various authors in this book.[1] For instance, in *Diaspora Representations and the Interweaving of Cultures*, we feature chapters such as Joseph Mclaren's "Tess Onwueme and Diaspora Representations in *The Missing Face*", which depicts characters that retain the western mode of speech as their non-African counterparts, but whose utterances convey their deep identity. Mwenya B. Kabwe, on the other hand, in "Performing Africa Differently: Articulations of Migrant Identity in a Re-imagining of Adrienne Kennedy's *Funnyhouse of A Negro*" situates a diaspora play in a South African context—in a way that foregrounds embodied utterance as opposed to the spoken word.

Performing the World into Being

Joanne Spooner, one of the contributors, writes that "culture is a mechanism of identification, a repository for people's sense of identity that requires constant re-affirmation through performance", and—

according to Homi Bhabha—it is the performativity in and of language that ensures that the narrative of the nation is carried out, and that the nation needs this narration in order to come into being (1990: 3). In *Performing America: Cultural Nationalism in American Theater* (1999), the editors Jeffrey Mason and Ellen Gainor explore in the introduction to the book how the theatrical representations of the United States has helped to shape the national identity of the country. They specifically demonstrate the role the theatre has played in the construction of American identity.

Thus it is valid to say that African theatre performs the African world, and through it the African identity, into being. This is mainly because of its nature and also because it is perceived in, and by, most African societies, as a cultural process and practice—it is not an activity that is outside of the normal things that people do or take part in, because African cultures demand of its people a certain amount or level of performance every once in while. When an individual is born, that individual performs or has others perform for, or on their behalf—whether it is their naming ceremony, puberty initiation, or rites of passage into a masquerade fraternity or women's associations. As the person gets older, they begin to perform themselves, supported by others, into new states of being. For example, if they become wealthy, they may acquire status as leader, chief etc. through engaging in further performances.

Finally, when the person dies, there are the rites of transition into the realm of the ancestors or the respected dead, who are often performed into being by the living as masquerades. In other words, performances are done on behalf of the dead person who becomes a passive participant in their own performance—just as they had been as a new-born baby at the first performance of their life. Whether one is an active or passive performer in their life performances, they remain or perform as themselves—this goes back to the idea of performativity in which the conventional rules of framing a performance are rendered inoperative in African theatre. They can also be seen as performing alternative realities into being, because they mark palpable changes or transformations in the lives of those involved.

African performances flow out of and back into society. They are time out of time and yet they remain, and are firmly anchored, within the moment of performance. This is because the distance between the performed reality (the performance) and the lived reality (society) is constantly negotiated and breached, so that the boundary between them is forever porous and therefore ultimately they remain as one. The audience, on the one hand, are themselves, yet on the other hand they are performing a role. However, they are very much aware that they are doing so—which is to say, they are never not themselves.

This is true of performers in a variety of African performance traditions, such as Theatre for Development, trance and possession rituals, and the masquerade performances. It is, therefore, the performative element of so many indigenous African performance practices and traditions that gives African theatre its manifest theatricality— African theatre has previously been referred to as a theatre that consciously embraces and broadcasts its theatricality (Okagbue, 2007: 181). The performative element carries the famed functional quality of African performance, because African peoples perform not just to entertain themselves, but they do so to also impact on their world—to question, understand, challenge, and ultimately order and reorder their world. They use the theatre to celebrate and affirm what is good and to also to censor, admonish, and hopefully correct behaviours perceived not to be good. Performance is the tool for negotiating the complexities and anxieties of existence, and it is the phenomenon of performativity that enables this to happen—African peoples, it can be said, perform to be.

The essays contained in this three-volume book attest to these transformative qualities and impact-driven imperatives of African theatre and performance. The broad range of traditions and practices, and cultural and national contexts covered in this collection demonstrates the breadth of styles of theatre which exist, and the fact that each theatre practice or form is more or less in dialogue—either of affirmation or confrontation with its society and culture, and informing and being informed by, and changing and being changed by the environment in which it exists. These qualities apply to African theatre on the continent and in its various manifestations in the African diasporas of the Caribbean, South America, the United States of America, and Canada. Thus, a great many of the essays in this collection look at a diverse range of theatre and performance practices from different parts of Africa and the African diasporas. The essays all suggest that these performances, in their different ways, engage in this process of performing the world into being through their performative articulations or exploration of the divergent African and African diaspora experiences of Africans or peoples of African descent.

It is the idea of the performances captured by the majority of the essays in these three books as performative engagements, which underlines the unity of the collection. The essays and the theatrical engagements and traditions which they discuss capture either the overall performative imperative which informs the type of theatre, or they record the performative moments when the actual transformation desired occurs or is expected to occur.

Themes and Approaches

Performative Inter-Actions in African Theatre explores three major themes, which are captured in the subtitles of each of the three books within the set. The first of the three books is subtitled: *Diaspora Representations and the Interweaving of Cultures*. This is followed by Book 2 which is subtitled: *Innovation, Creativity and Social Change,* and Book 3 is subtitled: *Making Space, Rethinking Drama and Theatre in Africa.* The volumes are written by a wide range of international scholars, thus topics are discussed with an in-depth critical vocabulary and focus appropriate for a publication written for an international readership—the contributors' backgrounds and global spread reflect our international focus in putting this book together.

The contributions, in their various ways, demonstrate the many advances and ingenious solutions adopted by African theatre practitioners in tackling some of the challenges arising from the adverse colonial experience, as well as the "one-sided" advance of globalisation. The contributions attest to the thriving nature of African theatre and performance, which in the face of these challenges has managed to retain its distinctiveness, while at the same time acknowledging, contesting, and appropriating influences from elsewhere into an aesthetic that is identifiably African. Consequently, we present the three books published under this title—*Performative Inter-Actions in African Theatre*—as a comprehensive exploration of the current state of African theatre and performance, both on the continent and diaspora.

In Book 1, *Diaspora Representations and the Interweaving of Cultures*, we present essays that show that even though the plays of the African diaspora acknowledge and pay homage to the cultures of *home* in the various locations around the world, they do not lose a sense of their Africanness in their various inter-actions. This sense of interweaving of cultures—without losing a sense of their indigenous African influences and sensibilities—is evident in the contributions that explore performances from the African diaspora, as well as those performances located on the continent that engage with this idea of interweaving in much the same way as their diaspora counterparts. Thus, the idea of *Diaspora Representations* attests to the notion that the diaspora—as we see it—is not solely located outside of the African continent itself, but can be found in those performances that engage performatively with the West in that process of articulating identity.

Book 2, *Innovation, Creativity and Social Change*, on the other hand, contains contributions that address performativity as a process— particularly in the context of theatre's engagement with social realities with the hope of instituting or achieving social change and the transformation of society. The innovativeness of some of the applied and community theatre practices explored within the book points to the ingenuity and adaptiveness of African theatre in a way that enables it to engage indigenous forms in the service of contemporary realities. This privileges an approach to theatre and performance that constantly redefines and reshapes itself, so as to remain relevant and in tune with contemporary realities in the quest for social change. The contributions deal with forms such as Theatre for Development, community and applied theatre, and indigenous juridical performances, as well as the use of indigenous performance forms by contemporary dramatists and performers to instigate change in society.

Finally, in Book 3, *Making Space, Rethinking Drama and Theatre in Africa*, we present essays that seek to reconceptualise notions of drama and theatre in Africa, and therefore redefine our understanding of the practice, role, and place they occupy in a constantly evolving society. Contributions in *Making Space, Rethinking Drama and Theatre in Africa* range from essays that explore notions of space in performance, to those that challenge the perceived orthodoxy of conventional forms and approaches to theatre.

The individual themes of each of the three books intersect at various points and consequently the overarching theme of all three is the fact that they are linked in their exploration of the performative and interactive nature of performance in Africa and the African diasporas. Thus in this concluding section of the introductory chapter, we go on to discuss the various approaches adopted by some of the contributors in the volumes in their attempts to engage with notions of performativity and inter-actions.

In Book 3, for instance, in his essay "Dreams Deferred: National Theatres in National Development", Osita Okagbue in arguing for the national theatres in Africa as institutions responsible for preserving, nurturing, and disseminating each nation's theatrical traditions and art forms, invokes the Owerri Igbo *mbari*. *Mbari* is understood as "a house of art" in which a group of young men and women of the community are selected to devote a period of time in utter seclusion. While in seclusion, they are tasked with using the process of "making" art to begin a programme of knowledge, communal engagement, and healing. The process of making the art is simultaneously the process of "healing and empowerment" for the community for whom, and in which, the *mbari* house is situated. The *Mbari* house and art are made and then abandoned, left to decay and fall apart. Thus, its efficacy is not in the art or the house that people behold, but rather in the selection of candidates and the process of making or constructing the house, as well as the art objects that adorn it.

Okagbue's essay, however, does not suggest that the impermanence of *mbari* be transferred to how African countries manage their national theatres, but rather it emphasises the idea that the usefulness of a national theatre is ultimately dependent on what happens, when it happens, and how it happens within it as an institution. In a similar vein, Benita Brown's essay in Book 1, which is titled "The *Òrìsà* Paradigm: An Overview of African-Derived Mythology, Folklore, and Kinaesthetic Dance Performatives", explores the jazz dance of the African diaspora in the United States of America—which she terms a "dance performative". In it she argues that the inspiration and modality of this dance performative affords its African-American participants the opportunity to be touched by the "Òrìsà". Brown's premise of jazz as a dance performative facilitates, for participants, a context and a moment for the recovery and embracement of their African ancestral past—through the *asé* (the Yoruba concept of power utterance to bring about change) that is generated, the individual participants are able to engage and come to terms with their current realities.

In much the same way, Krueger's chapter, "*Zef* / Poor White Kitsch Chique: South African Comedies of Degradation" (Book 3)—in looking at the new phenomenon of *Zef* derogatory comedy in South Africa—concludes that:

> within *Zef*'s mockery of poor white Afrikaner resides an attempt to come to terms with some of the unsettling qualities inherent in a new South African white identity… an identity which has had to reshape itself within the context of a hybrid culture.

We see thus in this performance how a character becomes a mode of appropriating and coming to terms with the past in order to move forward in the present. This idea of moving forward in the present is precisely what the *gacaca* court performances of Rwanda—the subject of the opening chapter of Book 2 entitled "Juridical Performatives: Public Versus Hidden Scripts and Transcripts"—illustrates. In this essay, Ananda Breed argues that the court hearings demonstrate the power of the performative utterance, and that the moment of confession, atonement, and reconciliation brings about healing for a community and country that is traumatised and still reeling from its experience of genocide and ethnic cleansing. The confessions serve as appeasement to those who had been wronged, and for those who perpetrated the wrongs, by confessing they own up and take responsibility for the crimes committed.

Annette Bühler-Dietrich's contribution in Book 2, "Burkina Faso: Theatre's Impact on Creating the Future" examines a range of Theatre for Development events and programmes that take place mainly around the capital, Ouagadougou, but also in other towns and villages. She equally argues that even the literary plays are geared toward making a transformational impact on the audience and thus playwrights have that in mind when they write, which means that the notion of "art for art's sake" has no place in such an environment.

The same attempt to use the theatre to create the future is the topic explored in Book 1 by Joanna Spooner in her chapter "Enacting the Nation: Transcultural, Performativity in the Construction of National Identity in *Juliush Siza* and *Moses, Citizen and Me*". Spooner shows in her essay how Thomas Dekker's *Juliush Siza*—a Krio translation of *Julius Ceasar* —is a political act that performatively serves as the process of imagining the Sierra Leonean nation, while *Moses, Citizen and Me* constitutes a re-enactment of the conception of the nation already imagined by Dekker in his play. Spooner's argument, therefore, is that the enactment of the nation can become performative, and that performance contributes to the construction of the nation and ultimately the national identity.

"Cultural Factors, Power Dynamics and Effective Theatre in HIV/AIDS Education in South Africa" found in Book 2 is the title of the chapter by Chijioke Uwah and Patrick Ebewo. In it, they examine theatre as an intervention in the fight against the HIV/AIDS pandemic, which has been decimating a sizeable number of the potentially productive population in South Africa. They argue that the theatre played a significant and successful role in the fight against apartheid because it was made from the grassroots. Consequently, they argue that the reason why the interventions against the spread of HIV/AIDS have not worked is not because theatre has lost its potential to be efficacious, but simply because of the practitioners' "inadequate knowledge of their target audiences' cultural norms and values" and the fact that they did not get the audience involved at the early stages of the theatre process.

So the choice of *Performative Inter-Actions in African Theatre* as a title for this book is not fortuitous. It was carefully chosen firstly because of the editors' awareness that the theatre traditions, styles, and forms found on the African continent and the African diasporas are predicated on the notion of performativity. And secondly, on the belief that in instituting art forms and practices, African peoples set up mechanisms, instruments, and contexts for engaging, examining, understanding, and affecting their worlds—by making the invisible visible and bringing the past into the present in order to predict and manage the future. Underpinning all of this is an understanding that whatever is said or done within the theatrical space, has the capacity to affect what happens in the world outside it because the boundary between the imagined world of the theatre and the world outside it are porous, in the same way that the boundary between the performer and spectator in indigenous African performances is deliberately made porous—always flexible with performer occasionally becoming spectator and vice versa.

References

Austin, J. L. (1962) *How to Do Things with Words.* Oxford: Clarendon Press.

Azuonye, N. (2003) "My e-Conversation with Esiaba Irobi." (Online). Available from: <http://www.sentinelpoetry.org.uk/magazine0203/page35.html> [Accessed 18 January 2011].

Bhabha, H. (1990) *Nation and Narration.* London: Routledge.

Bial, H. (ed). (2007) *The Performance Studies Reader,* 2nd edn. London: Routledge.

Blocker, J. (1999) *Where is Ana Mendieta?: Identity, Performativity, and Exile.* Durham and London: Duke University Press.

Butler, J. (1990) *Gender Trouble: Feminism and the Subversion of Identity.* London and New York: Routledge.

—. (1993) *Bodies that Matter: On the Discursive Limits of Sex.* London and New York: Routledge.

Harris, G. (1999) *Staging Feminisms: Performance and Performativity.* Manchester: Manchester University Press.

Jackson, S. (2004) *Professing Performance: Theatre in the Academy from Philology to Performativity.* Cambridge: CUP.

Loxley, J. (2007) *Performativity.* Oxon/ New York: Routledge.

Mason, J. and Gainor, E. (1999) *Performing America: Cultural Nationalism in American Theater.* Ann Arbor: The Michigan University Press.

Okagbue, O. (2007) *African Theatres and Performances.* London and New York: Routledge.

Otas, B. (2008) "An Interview with Oladipo Agboluaje." *The New Black Magazine,* [online] Available at: <http://www.thenewblackmagazine.com/view.aspx?index=1352> [Accessed 21 November 2012].

Parker, A. and Sedgwick, E. K. (eds.). (1995) *Performativity and Performance.* New York, London: Routledge.

Schechner, R. (2002) *Performance Studies: An Introduction.* London: Routledge.

CHAPTER ONE

IN SEARCH OF NEW PERFORMANCE SPACES: THEATRE PRACTITIONERS AND FM RADIO STATIONS IN KENYA

CHRISTOPHER JOSEPH ODHIAMBO

Introduction

In Kenya, the performing artist has always been nomadic—forever searching for performance spaces—and in the postcolonial Kenyan state this is even more so. In the pre-colonial period, however, there were some artists who were not mobile. These artists operated in defined and recognisable performance spaces. For instance, among the Luos of the Lake region of Kenya, the grandmother's house—known as *siwindhe*—was in the evenings, a designated performance space. Here the elderly members of the community initiated the young girls and boys into the ways of the community, as well as the art of oral performance. The same also happened in the grandfather's house—known as *duol*—where the young male adults were initiated into the ways of the community through oral performances especially on matters to do with manhood such as war, hunting and security. It is worth noting that the performances that took place in the *siwindhe* and *duol* were expressly didactic, though also entertaining.

Those who performed in these spaces were, however, non-professional performers and construed their roles as educators. However, the more professional performers, known as *jothum*, who play a range of musical instruments such as the *ohangla*, *nyatiti*, and *onanda*, traverse villages in the quest for spaces, where cultural activities and rituals take place and bring the community together—such as marriage ceremonies, funerals, beer parties, and installation of chiefs—where they can perform their art. With the invasion of colonial modernity, however, the use of these spaces for performances became restricted. This sense of "open space" was replaced with "confined government-supervised urban community halls, school halls, church buildings, theatre buildings with proscenium stage" (wa Thiong'o, 1981: 38).

In pre-colonial Kenya, performance space was unrestricted and the artist could perform in any "empty space" without any inhibition whatsoever. As Ngũgĩ wa Thiong'o rightly points out in regard to the way drama manifested itself in pre-colonial Kenya:

> ...it was not an isolated event: it was part and parcel of the rhythm of daily seasonal life of the community. It was an activity among other activities, often drawing its energy from those other activities. It was also entertainment in the sense of involved enjoyment; it was moral instruction; and it was also a strict matter of life and death and communal survival. This drama was not performed in special buildings set aside for the purpose. It could take place anywhere-wherever there was an empty space... "The empty space", among the people was part of that tradition. (wa Thiong'o, 1981: 37)

As mentioned earlier, the performance space in Kenya became problematic because it was no longer unrestricted in usage—especially with the intrusion of colonial modernity which disrupted the cultural practices that were accompanied by drama and theatre performances. Admittedly, the issue of performance space became even more problematic and complex in the postcolonial Kenyan state. For instance, the Kenya National Theatre as a performance space:

> remained the preserve of the British expatriate community even after Kenya had her own national anthem and national flag in 1963. It was run by a wholly expatriate governing council with the British Council retaining a representative many years after independence. (wa Thiong'o, 1981: 40)

But this domination of the official space by agents of the former colonial power was not the main problem. The use of performance spaces, whether formal or informal, was further complicated by the nature of the postcolonial state that emerged in Kenya. As wa Thiong'o would remind us:

> The performance space for prayers, funeral dirges, marriage ceremonies, naming tea-parties, family gatherings, sports, are dependent on issuance of a permit. Thus when the police break into any gathering and break up story-telling sessions in people's homes, they are absolutely within the law. Performances have to be contained in controllable enclosures, in licensed theatre buildings, in schools, especially, but not in open spaces where people reside. (wa Thiong'o, 1998: 69)

It was more than just the postcolonial state controlling and containing performance spaces in Kenya, however, because the physical geographical locations of most of these vestiges of colonialism were inaccessible to most audiences. As Richard Frost, (cited in Mwangola, 2008: 20), reports:

> The National Theatre was built where it was built because those who planned the scheme, including Thornly Dyer, the architect who designed the parliament Building and conceived of the Master plan of Nairobi wanted to build the National Theatre in the "snob area" of Nairobi… As it was not to be a working class theatre, it was built in the middle of well-to-do Nairobi… "people's theatres" could be established elsewhere, but the National Theatre and Cultural Centre were to be at the Centre of Nairobi.

The isolated, and isolating, geographical location of the Kenya National Theatre and Kenya Cultural Centre have had adverse economic implications for theatre practitioners who depend on box office sales for their income. They persistently perform to empty theatre houses which, as Frost indicates, are far removed from the proximity of their intended audiences who are mainly the working class population who cannot afford the cost of travel to these spaces. Yet the elite, who can afford to travel, are not interested in these popular performances.

Besides the problem of proximity, most of the theatre houses in Kenya are too expensive for theatre groups to hire. Many groups—apart from those performing school-set plays, where schools buy tickets and ferry their students to watch the shows—cannot recoup their overhead costs after paying the costs for the hire of the theatre. However, for many years the British Council Cultural Centre(s) auditoriums and French Cultural Centre in Nairobi—which are often accused, ironically, of cultural imperialism—became the preferred performance spaces for upcoming artists as they are considerably cheaper to hire and more accessible in terms of geographical proximity to ordinary residents of Nairobi. The theatre groups that perform in these spaces include: Falaki Arts (now known as Heartstrings Ensemble), Friends Theatre, Mbalamwezi, Fanaka Arts, Festival of Arts, and Uzinduzi Productions. The other alternative performance space was the University of Nairobi Education Theatre II, which readily opened its doors to a number of theatre groups from the early 1980s till the late 1990s.

The control and containment of the performance space in the postcolonial Kenyan state is not restricted only to the more physical theatre spaces, but also extends to virtual technologically mediated spaces such as radio and television. Before 1992, the state-owned radio and television station, Voice of Kenya (VOK)—which later became known as

Kenya Broadcasting Corporation (KBC)—determined through a rigorous censorship board, the kind of radio and television dramas that could be aired to the public. Only apolitical plays (perceived by the board as morally correct) and developmental message oriented drama and comedies that were perceived as uncritical of the government were aired. However, this situation changed dramatically in 1992 with the end of the cold war era and the fall of the Berlin Wall.

The authoritarian regime of the then president, Daniel Arap Moi, conceded to both internal and external pressure to open up the democratic space, amending Section 2A of the constitution that had previously denied Kenyans a number of freedoms and rights, such as the freedom of assembly and expression. The opening up of the democratic space heralded a more liberalised society: economically, socially, culturally, and politically. This liberalisation also saw the expansion of both physical and virtual performance spaces in the postcolonial Kenyan state. Theatre, especially the awareness-raising types, could now find their way into the previously restricted "open spaces" in various communities. For instance, the Centre for Law and Research International (CLARION) was able to tour its civic education forum theatre productions to different parts of the country to conscientise the populace on their rights as citizens.

Initially, this expansion of the democratic space, and the consequent liberalisation of the physical performance and virtual spaces, adversely affected the proscenium stage theatre. Many of its practitioners shifted to developmental and educational theatre where they were commissioned to do plays, which guaranteed them a more predictable income stream from international and non-governmental organisations. Many others also "migrated" to the new FM radio stations that were fast appearing. For instance, actors such as Walter Mongare (aka Nyambane or Baby Nyams), Daniel Ndambuki (aka Churchill), Jackie Nyaminde (aka Wilbroda), Felix Odiwuor (aka Jalang'o), James Chiaji (aka Mshamba), Chris Okinda, Larry Asego, and Cindy Ogana moved to FM radio stations as presenters.

It is the effect of this shift of theatre practitioners to FM radio's virtual space as a performance space that the rest of this chapter will focus on. I am specifically interested in how the technologies of radio and mobile telephony have combined to create a theatre of the everyday life in Kenya. As such, I am not going to belabour the vast impact of technology in the development of theatre/drama performances, whose influence of course can never be underestimated.

FM Radio and the Theatre of Everyday Life

The kind of radio theatre that I am referring to here is not the conventional radio theatre/drama that depends on a well-written script and follows the techniques of radio drama and theatre. This is an emerging form of radio theatre performance that is highly discursive and eclectic in its orientation; it depends largely on the versatility of the presenter as a performer, more like the narrator in an oral performance, who is a storyteller, singer, commentator, and social critic. To conceptualise this theatre, I draw heavily from Allan Read's (1993) ideas on theatre and the everyday life; Hans-Thies Lehmann's (2006) ideas on postdramatic theatre; Augusto Boal's (1979) ideas on Forum Theatre, Newspaper Theatre, Invisible Theatre, and the notion of the Joker; and Wole Soyinka's (1988) thoughts on the survival patterns of theatre in indigenous African cultures.

An idea to which I will return later in this chapter has to do with what I consider to be the paradox of survival of the proscenium stage theatre. This is because, when faced with the threat of extinction as a result of the growth in entertainment technology, the proscenium stage theatre had to adapt to ensure its survival. At this juncture, I turn to Soyinka's (1988) thoughts on the survival patterns of indigenous oral art forms to demonstrate how the emerging FM radio "theatre of everyday life" has indeed given a new lease of life to indigenous oral performances and other non-text-based theatres, such as the forum and invisible theatre varieties. Soyinka argues that art forms are influenced by new environments and that these art forms in return either influence or appropriate, perhaps subversively, their new environments.

Technology is obviously one such environment that appears as a threat to a variety of physical space oriented theatre and oral performances. In fact, the migration of proscenium stage theatre practitioners to the virtual space of FM radio reiterates Soyinka's view that: "we begin to understand now why dating the origin of African drama, locating it in a specific event, time and place is an impossible one" (1983: 203). For instance, when listening to a performance on an FM radio station one easily gets a sense that this is actually an indigenous oral performance. An example of this comes from KBC FM radio station channel 92.5's daily programme known as *Uzani Mkuu (Serious Matter)*, usually aired from 6.00 am to 10.00 am, Monday to Friday, and presented by two "presenter-performers": Boniface Mzame (aka Bonny Bonny) and Cynthia Anyango (aka Cynthy Cynthy).

One particular morning, Bonny Bonny and Cynthy Cynthy were performing a story that explored the theme of teenage pregnancy and parental responsibility. The two, using the relay narration mode of rendition, narrate the story of a young girl who is impregnated by an equally young boy. Both of them are still in school. The girl informs the boy of her condition and the boy immediately denies responsibility. The girl gathers courage and informs her mother about her condition and, predictably, her mother gets extremely furious at her, but finally decides to go and confront the boy and his parents. As the mother explains what their son had done to her daughter to the boy's parents, they listen with a lot of concern and, in fact, admonish their son for such an irresponsible act and behaviour. But there is a twist in the plot of this story. After the girl's mother has left, the boy's parents immediately become excited and begin to praise their son for proving that he is a "real man". The story ends at this point with the radio presenter-performers inviting listeners to give their comments and share their own experiences.

What is profoundly significant in all this is the performance strategy deployed by the two radio presenter-performers to render this story. They narrated the story through the deployment of different tonal inflections to help their listeners imagine the characters. For instance, they employed role-play, mimicked speech mannerisms to give specific identities to their characters, and improvised using their voices as instruments. They consciously selected relevant and appropriate music to enhance the theme under discussion, and also used proverbs and riddles to enhance the moral of the story. At the end of the story, through call-ins using mobile phone service providers, they created a kind of forum theatre-type discussion to help resolve the issue.

Listening to *Uzani Mkuu*, memories of indigenous oral performances and Boalian Forum theatre techniques are immediately rekindled from the way the narration techniques, interactive debate, and the joker figure were deployed. Thus it is possible for one to deduce, like Soyinka, that the old art forms have actually appropriated this new technologically mediatised and mediated space. This appropriation of a new space by theatre practitioners working as presenter-performers in FM radio resonates very much with Hans-Thies Lehmann's concept of "palimpsests" in which old materials are reused in new theatre environments and spaces. This example, to a considerable degree, confirms Soyinka's observation,

> that the temporary historic obstacles to the flowering of a particular form sometimes lead to its transformation into other media of expression, or even the birth of totally different groups. (Soyinka, 1988: 145)

It is clear from the picture that emerges, of oral performance elements in *Uzani Mkuu*, that indigenous oral performance forms have appropriated the technologically mediated virtual space and are actually flowering. This observation should put to rest the anxieties of one of Kenya's foremost oral narrative performers, Amadi kwaa Atsiaya, who claims that modern performance spaces have failed to accommodate the complexity and dynamic participatory nature of indigenous oral performance. He laments that:

> Sigana is therefore confronted with challenges in terms of physical space because the conventional spaces do not provide for the oneness of audience and performer... Instead it provides for a situation where there will necessarily be a clear distinction between those who are watching and those who are performing. (kwaa Atsiaya, 2008: 53)

On the contrary, this oneness is made possible through the virtual space created by the convergence of the presenter-performers and their participatory audiences on the radio, using mobile phone calls and short text messages (SMS).

FM radio as a virtual performance space, complemented with mobile telephony, extends the possibilities of oral performances, and encourages the audience to become more involved because they must try and "see" the verbal utterances through their mind's eyes. This argument is affirmed by Soyinka's own, when he reminds us that:

> ...drama, like any other art form is created and executed within a specific physical environment. It naturally interacts with that environment, is influenced by it, influences that environment in turn and acts together with that environment in the larger and far more complex history of society. (Soyinka, 1988: 134)

Nearly all of the FM radio stations frame their morning shows à la the structure of the indigenous oral narrative performance. The presenter-performers of these FM radio shows use the techniques of the narrator in an oral narrative performance to convey their stories, using riddles, proverbs, and songs. The presenter-performer, like the narrator, seems to be aware that they are performing to an audience even if that audience is invisible. Through call-ins they are then able to involve their listeners in their performances. This structure was pioneered by the duo of Kiss 100 FM presenter-performers, Walter Mongare (aka Nyambane) and Caroline Mutoko. Kiss 100 FM was the first radio station to introduce actors from the popular stand-up comedy theatre company, Reddykulass and another, Jimmi Gathu, from the Mbalamwezi Theatre Players.

Kiss 100 FM's morning programme is instructively christened the *Big Breakfast Show*. This obviously suggests that it is implicated in some kind of performance. Like most other programmes in the morning, it runs from 6.00 am to 10.00 am on weekdays. The show was initially presented by Larry Asego and Caroline Mutoko who were later joined by Felix Odiwuor (aka Jalang'o). Asego later left Kiss 100 FM for Classic FM. Like Asego, Odiwuor is a renowned proscenium stage theatre actor. Odiwuor is a member of Culture Spill and Oturo Ng'ede Productions that perform plays mainly in the Dholuo language, while Asego is a member of the Heartstrings Ensemble. The Kiss 100 FM shows comprise a variety of oral art forms, news items taken from newspapers, gossips, dialogues, and "quasi forum theatre". All the performances are derived from the daily experiences of Kenyans. The shows would usually begin with a "quasi drama" structured around the conversation of the three presenter-performers (Jalang'o, Asego and Mutoko) on topics derived from news stories taken from one of the daily newspapers. Following their initial dialogue on a topic, they would then invite their listeners to join them in the dialogic drama. The interesting dimension of this dialogic drama is the manner in which the listeners who join the dialogue naturally become part of it by taking specific roles and playing along. In this drama the presenter-performers parody, impersonate, and mimic identifiable personalities in society.

As well as the "quasi drama" that ensues, the morning shows include the use of proverbs, gossip, and reworking of popular music to enhance their themes. The show also includes the "inside story". This is usually a brief news item from a newspaper that most readers would ordinarily ignore. The "Joker" in the show narrates the story, exaggerating certain aspects to elicit and evoke humour and laughter in the listeners/audience. The listeners are then invited to respond to the story through the narration of similar stories from their own experiences. The other aspect of the show is known as *muchene ya Nairobi*. *Muchene* is the Gikuyu word for gossip. This section is also taken from the daily newspapers and is usually a narration of an aberrant act by some important person or celebrity. After presenting this gossip with lots of humour, once again the listeners are also invited to "perform" gossips from their neighbourhoods and work places. This segment of the show is mainly meant to poke fun at those whose moral conduct is contrary to societal expectations.

Not all the material performed in the show is for amusement, entertainment, and ridicule. A number of them are usually framed in the form of "intervention drama". It is in this sense that I argue that these performances can be read and interpreted, drawing on Boal's ideas and practices of theatre of the oppressed—specifically his forum theatre, newspaper theatre, and invisible theatre. A few examples will suffice to illustrate. The case that I mentioned earlier, of teenage pregnancies, is an apt example of forum theatre. In this particular instance, after the story had been performed, members of the public were invited to participate in the discussion and to assist in resolving the problem of teenage pregnancy. This approach is very close to Frèire's problem solving pedagogy and Boal's forum theatre technique.

The FM radio version of newspaper theatre, mainly those by Kiss 100 FM, begins with an exaggerated rendition of a lead story in one of the daily newspapers. The presenter-performers begin by discussing the issue in a section they call the "burning issue of the day". For instance, the debate on whether the perpetrators of post-election violence should be tried at the International Criminal Court (ICC) at The Hague or locally in Kenya, was an issue that elicited a lot of interest and emotion in the media for many weeks. The presenter-performers took opposing views on the issue and invited members of the public to contribute their own views. Another topical issue has been the question of whether legislators should pay taxes as stipulated in the new constitution or not. The presenter-performers selected stories reported in the newspapers, of those legislators who are opposed to the payment of tax according to the constitution, and invited the public to participate in dialogic drama on the issue.

The invisible theatre technique is a strategy mainly used by the presenter-performers of Easy FM radio, Bernard Otieno and Maurice Ochieng (aka Mudomo Baggy). Their show is framed in such a way that one presenter-performer would remain in the studio, while the other would be out on the streets. The two presenter-performers would select a topic based on a major issue of national interest. They would then argue about the issue and, predictably, refuse to see the issue from the same perspective. It is at the moment when the two fail to agree that the performer in the studio would ask his co-performer to go to the people in the streets and ask them about their views/opinions on the issue. Interestingly, members of the public would often not be aware that their views were being aired live on radio. As such, they would give very sincere and objective views on the subject under discussion.

What is important, therefore, is the way that these theatre practitioners—who have shifted from the proscenium stage to the virtual space of FM radio—have appropriated the technology mediated and mediatised space, and aptly used it to create a new theatre of everyday life using the skills and techniques from theatre, à la palimpsests and bricolage. This kind of theatre resonates with Alan Read's idea of the role of theatre in everyday life, especially when he asks if theatre can still have value when divorced from everyday life. Read perfectly answers his own question, which I find profound in understanding this emerging FM radio theatre of everyday life, when he explains that:

> Everyday life is the meeting ground for all activities associated with human-work, play, friendship and the need to communicate, which includes the expressions of theatre. Everyday life is thus full of potential— it is the "everyday" which habitually dulls sense of life's possibilities. Theatre when it is good enables us to know the everyday in order to better live everyday life. (Read, 1993: 1)

According to Read, theatres of the everyday are implicit rather than explicit. He argues that it is the discreteness of this sort of theatre that makes it significant. This emerging FM radio theatre:

> poaches on everyday life for its content, relationships, humour, surprise, shock, intimacy and voyeurism. It takes from unities of time and space, domestic setting, landscapes and speech patterns that are often identifiable because they are drawn from the everyday life, and are celebrated precisely because they are somehow true to that world. (Read, 1993: 47)

FM radio theatre, therefore, appropriates anecdotes, gossips, quizzes, stories, hip hop, rap, proverbs, riddles, improvisations, role play, ordinary conversations, forum theatre techniques, invisible theatre, newspaper stories, and news to critique and comment on social, economic, cultural, gender, racial, linguistic, and ethnic issues facing contemporary postcolonial Kenyan society.

Conclusion

Having described this form of theatre that has emerged and flourished as a result of theatre practitioners migrating to the virtual space of FM radio, I now conclude by exploring the paradox of this migration. From an interview with Obilo Ng'ong'o, a Kenyan actor with the Heartstrings Ensemble Theatre, I realised that there is a strong symbiotic relationship between FM radio theatre and the renaissance of the proscenium stage theatre in Kenya—particularly in the capital city, Nairobi. This resurgence in proscenium stage theatre is largely due to the work of the FM radio presenter-performers, most of whom are also renowned practitioners of live theatre in Kenya. They have developed mechanisms by which FM radio theatre and proscenium stage theatre feed off each other. The FM radio presenters take ideas from stage theatre performances which they use in their radio theatre shows. Obilo Ng'ong'o, in the interview conducted in June 2011, remarks that responses from their audiences indicate that a number of them go to watch live proscenium stage performances in other to see some of their favourite FM radio presenter-performers on stage.

More importantly, many of the presenter-performers who continue to perform on the stage use their influence and popularity to publicise and popularise the productions that they are involved in through the FM radio stations. For instance, the Kiss 100 FM presenter, Jalang'o, would always ask his listeners not to forget to go and watch any play at the Kenya Cultural Centre where he performs. The same applies to Asego, who performs with the Heartstrings Ensemble. Because of their celebrity status, it can be argued that these presenter-performers have managed, to some extent, to bring back audiences to the theatre venues. However, Obilo Ng'ong'o—in the interview—argues that working in radio stations help these presenter-performers (who also double as stage actors) to understand the kind of theatre that their audiences would love to watch. He explains:

> By this time it was almost obvious that a different kind of audience wanted to watch this kind of plays presented in pedestrian English, Swahili Sheng and other common languages, portraying daily Kenyan situations with characters much like them [Kenyan audience]. This success did not come without casualties. Many theatregoers and critics found these shows to be "below them". It was a risk from the beginning, knowing that some of Heartstrings audiences were ardent supports of British farce and "strictly scripted" plays. Critics saw no apparent structure in the new genre. It is true, the scenes are somehow not connected, the storyline is sometimes vague, too many characters on stage forcing actors to play many different roles, too noisy, different plays looked similar etc. Yet as many [audiences] "divorced" Heartstrings, many more were streaming into the theatre [to see them]. (Ng'ong'o, 2011)

Thus to echo Soyinka, despite new and threatening environments, a work of art will always survive—either as a new genre or as part of that new environment. At a superficial level, it may be easy to claim that the radio, as a new performance space, has invaded and threatened the survival of proscenium theatre and oral narrative performance, but a critical analysis of the situation actually reveals that the converse is true.

References

Boal, A. (1979) *Theater of the Oppressed*. London: Pluto

kwaa Atsiaya, A. (2008) "Sigana and the Fight for Performance Space in Kenya: A Case for Indigenous Theatre in Kenya." *Getting Heard. (Re) Claiming Performance Space in Kenya*. Ed. Kimani Njogu. *Art, Culture and Society* 3: pp. 45–56.

Lehmann, H-T. (2006) *Postdramatic Theatre*. Transl. Karen Jurs-Munby. London/New York: Routledge.

Mwangola, M. (2008) "Njia Panda: Kenyan Theatre in Search of Identity." *Getting Heard: (Re) Claiming Performance Space in Kenya*. Ed. Kimani Njogu. *Art, Culture & Society* 3: pp. 1–24.

Ng'ong'o, O. (2011) Interview by C. J. Odhiambo. Eldoret, Kenya. 20 June 2011.

Odhiambo, C. J. (2006a) "From Siwindhe to Theatre Space: Paradigm Shift in the Performance of Oral Narratives in Kenya." *Our Landscapes, Our Narratives*. Eds. Indagasi, Wasamba, and Nyamasyo. Nairobi: KOLA. pp. 22–16.

—. (2006b) "Accentuating FM Radio Stations." *Jahazi* 1(1): pp. 15–20.

—. (2007) "Reading FM Radio Stations in Kenya: Opening a Pandora's Box." *Cultural Production and Social Change in Kenya*. Eds. Kimani Njogu and G. Olouch-Olunya. *Art Culture and Society* 1: pp. 151–161.

—. (2008a) "Colonising Space: Interrupting Usualness Through Civic Intervention Theatre." *Jahazi* 1(3): pp.44–47.

—. (2008b) "Circulation of Media Texts and Identity (De) Constructions in Postcolony." *Culture, Performance and Identity*. Ed. Kimani Njogu. *Art, Culture & Society* 2: pp. 131–144.

—. (2011) "From Diffusion to Dialogic Space: FM Radio in Kenya." *Radio Publics and Communities in Africa: Shared Pasts, Shared Futures*. Eds. Liz Gunner, Dumisani Moyo, and Dina Ligaga. Johannesburg: Wits University Press.

Read, A. (1993) *Theatre and Everyday Life: An Ethics of Performance*. London: Routledge.

Soyinka, W. (1988) "Theatre in African Traditional Cultures: Survival Patterns." *Art, Dialogue and Outrage: Essays on Literature and Culture*. Ibadan: New Horn Press Ltd.

wa Thiong'o, N. (1981) *Decolonising the Mind. The Politics of Language in African Literature*. London: James Currey; Nairobi: EAEP.

—. (1998) "Enactments of Power: The Politics of Performance Space." *Pen Points, Gun Points and Dreams. Towards a Critical Theory of Arts and State in Africa*. Oxford: Clarendon Press.

CHAPTER TWO

RE-CONTEXTUALISING *SPACE* USE IN INDIGENOUS AFRICAN COMMUNAL PERFORMANCE

VICTOR UKAEGBU

Introduction

One of the controversies in performance discourse is the application of an aesthetic framework from one tradition on another to which it is unrelated, without acknowledging that any similarity between the different systems are either accidental or coincidental. The theatrical transfer and imposition described here accounts for the unfortunate misinterpretation of cultural texts and performances that Soyinka (1988), Bharucha (1993), Balme (1999), and many other commentators have blamed for the misapplication of concepts in some postcolonial theatre practices and intercultural adaptations that seek to re-create the space and setting of the original for a new target audience (see also: Pavis, 1992 and 1996; and Ukaegbu, 2004). Similar misidentifications and misinterpretations occur frequently when Western spatial conventions are applied to the interpretation of space use and stage/audience relationship in indigenous African performances, most especially in communal performances where the requirement for overt mass participation (of which there are various kinds) calls for active stage and participant interactions, freedom of movement, and flexibility in stage businesses.

The differences alluded to here are logical and cultural. The aesthetic peculiarities and proxemic constructs of indigenous African communal performances, and their designs, locations, and uses are predicated primarily on cosmological conditions, such as a spatial construct that would—depending on the purpose—facilitate: *communitas* (Turner, 1974; Okagbue, 1987 and 2007) between a community and the forces of its universe; create a special, supra-physical, metaphysical atmosphere for the meeting of different but related essences; or temporarily transform the community, or parts of it, for a special encounter or re-enactment in which stage actions and behaviours, regarded as extra-ordinary, point to functions beyond the performance event itself. In such performances, space as a mere presentation platform and venue as a physical architectural structure—as used in modern Western and contemporary African theatres —are both un-representative and inadequate.

Performance Space as Cultural Construct

The ephemerality of performance and the physical limitations of space allow contemporary performance practitioners to present dramatic content without the requirement to re-produce the world of the unfolding drama in its exactitude. However, this cannot be said of indigenous performances where, in most instances, the aim is to re-produce the world, as well as to re-enact and to engage it as truthfully as possible. As a result, while contemporary performances may be content with presenting spatial arrangements by deploying what Chris Balme has called "signs and floating signifiers" in a "semiotic sense" (1999: 5), indigenous African performances aim for *"physical performance conditions"* in keeping "with indigenous spatial concepts" (Balme, 1999: 227) in which spaces are used for their cosmological, cultural, and archaeological associations.

For a long time, performance criticism has viewed spatial constructs of indigenous African forms and their contemporary counterparts with the same critical lenses, without conceding that while the terms "space" and "venue" derive essentially from modern performance discourse, they rarely describe the ambience and spatial relationship between performers and participants in indigenous forms in the same way as they do for modern contemporary forms. In some communities it may be part of the ritual requirement to re-enact specified episodes of socio-sacral performances in specific locales, such as: shrines and sacred groves, or beside sacred trees and rivers. Such locales may be described as spots within the performance space, rather than as venue(s).

Spaces and venues in indigenous communal performances reinforce cosmological unity of the performing community. Their locations and designs are predicated more on socio-sacral considerations and functional purposes—some of which have already been alluded to—and less on aesthetic unity and audience convenience. Even in instances where performances are driven essentially by performer/participant interactions, or are staged in confined and specified locations as stated, indigenous communal African performance spaces may combine any number of spatial factors, from the symbolic and metaphysical to the archaeological, pragmatic, and purely aesthetical, but command little of the overarching premium on audience convenience that contemporary dramatic forms generally espouse. Conceptually, space use in indigenous African performance aims for an inclusive experience—one in which, despite the obvious ephemerality and fictiveness of the moment, community members are framed as active participants in their own socio-sacral, archaeological, and metaphysical universe. The type of immersive spatial construct described here leads participants to the multi-level engagement and experience of the sensory, the tactile, and the physical, that is a defining feature of communal African performance.

This integrated and inclusive approach to performance experience is incidentally what Antonin Artaud, Jerzy Grotowski and Augusto Boal, and arguably, Peter Brook, were aiming for when they used staging techniques to draw attention to the separation of the senses in Western theatre and the need for their reintegration in production strategies and in audience experiences (see: Artaud, 1964; Grotowski cited in Wolford and Shechner, 2001; and Boal cited in Cohen-Cruz and Schutzman, 2006).

Indigenous and contemporary African performances subscribe to different spatial constructs. Therefore, subjecting space use in indigenous performances to the same analytical criteria as that used for contemporary performances is an aesthetic imposition on the former that needs re-visiting. Indigenous performance spaces in Africa communicate and reinforce cosmological unity and the universe of the presenting community. They are more than architectural buildings and spaces—such sites and locales are chosen for more than pragmatic reasons and are used specifically for performances because of their "mythical symbolism" (Balme, 1999: 232). They are not mere theatrical or narrative aids used to embellish and reinforce plots. They have cultural meanings and play active parts in the unfolding performances, and are, thus, significant "actants" (Hilton, 1987: 29) that contribute to the atmosphere and meaning of performances.

The association of spaces and venues with "actants" is very important in indigenous performances, such as masking, where presentations assimilate people and objects (animate and inanimate) both within and outside locales and spots of action, as well as along thoroughfares close to these sites. According to Julian Hilton:

> anything as well as any person can become an actant, a performer. The actant may be anthropomorphic …but it may be an article of clothing, or a place. (Hilton, 1987: 29)

Spatial arrangements are used in indigenous performances, not necessarily to demarcate the stage from the audience, but to enable "actors to run in and out of the audience" (Soyinka, 1988: 5) in the course of their performance, as well as to enhance audience's overall participation. Space and venue hardly describe the sort of "spaces" used in indigenous African performances or what happens in them. The absence of architectural buildings on which Balme and Carlson predicate their definition of modern performance spaces—suggests a different reading and one that will significantly come close to approximating the actant role played by space in these performances.

Balme's (1999) and Carlson's (1989) arguments that it is more appropriate to use architectural building and physical alteration of the landscape to define modern performance spaces are valid for more than just semantic reasons. Firstly, the arguments have important cultural resonance in indigenous African performances, where—whether present or absent—architecturally constructed spaces alone neither capture nor locate the entire cosmic ambience of a community. Secondly, architectural structures replicate only partially, "the wider context of the interface between performance space and surrounding environment" (Balme, 1999: 229)—such buildings, whether permanent or temporary, are important in indigenous African performances if they are built specifically for the overarching communal event or re-enactment of which they are a constituent part, and will continue to serve beyond the specific performance event.

In indigenous African performances, the relationship between dramatic content and structure is interwoven to reflect and reinforce what Una Chaudhuri has described as "deeply ingrained convictions about the mutually constructive relations between people and place" (2000: xii). Temporary structures may be required and built for a performance, and be preserved and used thereafter by the performance group or society that built them. Their fates and sacral importance are linked closely with the archaeological, mythological, and ecological histories of the communities that own them, or to special groups with which they are associated.

Negotiating the Performative Landscape: Cultural Site vs. Performance Space

Indigenous African communal performance spaces are cultural sites—a cultural site connotes a locale or location inclusive of the physical objects, the socio-sacral activities, and rituals and ritualised actions associated with it. Cultural sites are liminal spaces, physical constructs that reinforce the metaphysical relationships between place, performers, participants, and performance activities. Pearson and Shanks point out that in performances that operate "in a liminal space or hetertopia" (2001: 53),one of the functions of space—its design and use—is to negotiate "the identities of people and things" (2001: 54). Contemporary performance spaces may communicate existential ideas and information, yet their remits for negotiating group and cultural identities are far less important as socio-sacral entities in comparison to the role that cultural sites perform in African communities where site and locale are used for more than just aesthetic reasons, especially in socio-sacral performances.

I am referring here to the fact that participants need to also experience performance sites and locales for socio-cultural reasons, and that where they are in relation to displays determine their experience of place (Chaudhuri, 2000). According to Pearson and Shanks:

> Site, as concept, must be connected with place and locale, as the natural and cultural are entwined in a true ecology which moves beyond these familiar dualisms... site is as much a temporal as spatial concept—landscapes are enfolded; scenography works with the multidimensional temporality of memory, event and narrative. (2001: 55)

Indigenous performances are rooted in a society's universe. A community's performers and participants attend them with some knowledge of the narrative and are usually aware of the content and contexts of their supporting myths and legends. As a result:

> the audience comes to performance with a grid of pre-understandings which are partly unconscious or non-discursive, but are also contingent upon autobiography. (Pearson and Shanks, 2001: 64)

In practice, performance narratives:

> may intersect with the narrative of personal identity. Audiences experience the performance in a state of preparedness which derives from past experiences and the way in which they have chosen to order them and accord them significance. (Pearson and Shanks, 2001: 64)

The locations and sites are not de-sacralised, and even when the ritual threshold is deliberately lowered or raised to accommodate special circumstances, the locations maintain their power over proceedings—retaining, as it were, their ritual status and significance. In other words, rather than the separation of ritual purpose and social aesthetics that contemporary theatre spaces and venues entail, indigenous performances operate in liminal sites and locales with their own aesthetic and cognition codes, interpretation modes, and processes for generating meaning—that is, the meaning of performances and their associated stage businesses are inseparable from the cultural significance of the spaces and locales where they take place.

Pearson and Shanks' description of the connection between performance activities and locales as "a spectrum of strategies, practices and procedures which attend to questions of real-time presentation and representation" (2001: 55) reflects the uses and significance of cultural sites in indigenous African performances in which—while the purpose is not necessarily to distinguish reality from its representation—dramatic fiction, communal ceremony, and ritual re-enactments may use the same locations and spaces and aim for the same socio-sacral atmosphere.

The fact that a large number of indigenous performances incorporate itinerant stages means that performers are neither restricted to one space or arena, nor are theatrical and social meanings entirely dependent on the spatial arrangement and architectural structures we have come to associate with modern dramas staged in the confines of theatre buildings and conventional performance spaces. Indigenous African performances opt for the freedom of open sites and various locales in which performers traverse time and create meaning in no specific order, in the assurance that participants know the story-lines, know how to make meaning out of the presentations, and can determine how and when to participate.

Any number of features, from the content and function of a performance to the location of a shrine and audience involvement, may alter the spatial dynamic to the point of moving the show between different locations. Richard Schechner is, indeed, correct that the aesthetics of open air, environmental performances—like the ones described here—"is built on systems of interaction, on the ability of coherent wholes to include contradictory parts" (1994: xix). Spatial flexibility influences presentation and reception so that "the frames" of a presentation "may change during a single performance, transforming an event into something unlike what it started out" (Schechner, 1994: xix). The performances are communal undertakings to which people respond in diverse ways. The actions of performers and participants de-stabilise spatial boundaries while the reception strategy requires a space code that accommodates multiple locales and sites and even imponderable contradictions. Total visibility may once have been a feature of all theatre spaces, as Chaudhuri (2000) has pointed out, but as important as this factor may be, the spatial arrangements for indigenous performances are not determined by geometry but by geography and "archaeology" (Pearson and Shanks, 2001).

In many respects, indigenous African performers and participants do not only collude in what Pearson and Shanks (2001) would regard as making and documenting archaeological acts that are both temporal and archetypal—their actions may be symbolic or real and may embody important ritual meanings, but they are designed to align the purpose and overall meaning of presentations with the physical and metaphysical landscapes. The performers and participants are like nomads and ancient shamans who traverse their geographical terrains, "using points and locations to define paths rather than places" (Cresswell, 1997: 364 cited in Pearson and Shanks, 2001: 149). Space in these performances designates site and place and, in ritual displays in particular, the entire community becomes a performance place in which—although locales may be categorised on their importance—performers and participants use them to link together, the human and other worldly entities and zones that comprise their universe. Going forward, an analysis of two performances will provide useful clues to the cultural significance of performance sites and locales.

Performing Community: Community as Performance Place

Charles Gore's (1998) study of the configuration of shrines in modern-day Benin City in Nigeria highlights the performance by members of the *Ohen* priestly cult, and links their personal shrines to the many communal shrines spread over the city. This spatial arrangement, comprising of numerous personal and community shrines used as staging places, challenges conventional use of the term "venue" to describe place, arena, and staging site in indigenous African performances.

The *Ohen* is a priestly cult to which qualifying members of the Benin society may belong following application, approval, and a long period (between three and five years) of instruction from established, practising *Ohens*. As part of their training and initiation, the *Ohen* are required to perform publicly at many times and occasions, utilising one or more of the major components of the group's performance repertoire (singing, oratorical chants, dance, or the special *Ohen* costume) to demonstrate their pre-eminence in skills developed over the period of training and apprenticeship, and their close affinity to the spirit world. The public presentations are a requirement for becoming an *Ohen*. On the days in question, each trainee *Ohen* prepares his shrine, costumes himself, and ties a young yellow palm frond on his wrist to distinguish himself from other members of the public. Sometimes, *Ohens* travel from place to place performing to set music (as part of their training in the *Ohen* dance choreography/music score) and engage in other performative acts prescribed by the cult.

In effect, what we have here is not only the entire breadth of the city functioning as a performance space, the personal shrines of performing *Ohens* serve as specific performance sites within the wider performance locale. With each *Ohen* and his supporting cast of participants taking their acts to different parts of the town, sometimes with up to twenty or more *Ohens* presenting simultaneously at various locations across the city, participants and community members are able to criss-cross to various arenas of action. The information exchanged by participants reinforces participants' expectations and interactions with performers, and provides a unique reception experience that is possible only in such extensive, non-localised settings. The combined impact of interchanges and exchanges between participants and visitors to different *Ohen* shrines and along the road, and those of the happenings in various locales, create a staging, reception, and performer/participant dynamic that is totally different from what people experience in venues in contemporary performances.

The second example comes from Ogwa, a town about twelve miles from Owerri, the capital city of Nigeria's Imo State. *Ako Otuo* is a community cleansing and redressive ritual festival celebrated by the Ochii community in Ogwa. The festival is open to everyone and is designed to purge the community of bottled-up tensions, anger, animosities, resentments, quarrels and disunity, and enmities for which individuals and the community itself require cleansing in a ritual act of public expiation. There are many sides to the four-day festival, but the two most performative aspects are the ritual cursing that involves women and girls of all ages and the climactic ritual cleansing of the community leading to the hurling of physical representations or symbols of evil on the huge stem of the ritual Akwu tree in the *Ako Otuo* curses. Of the two aspects, the ritual cursing is spread throughout the community, while the ritual cleansing starts in the community square and proceeds to the market square before terminating at the community shrine. There are no prescribed costumes for the former as it is open to everyone interested in the performance and in the attendant festivities, while the latter—the ritual cleansing—requires special white costumes worn by the female performers and worshippers of the local deity, *Ezealaelu*.

During the ritual cursing, pairs of women stand opposite each other and hurl verbal abuses, slurs, and provocative accusations at each other. The liminal space and temporary suspension of all associated social censures allow performers and participants to hurl imagined, suspected, and real accusations and slanders at each other. The opponents could be siblings, the subjects of abuse could be families, personalities, behaviours, and actions to which opponents (who may actually be best friends) may be associated with or suspected of, or they may be the products of an abuser's flight of imagination. Nothing is held against anyone at the end, the most unimaginable things and ideas about somebody may be spread, with participants goading the verbal combatants on to the most alarming, incredulous curses. The abuses and curses are uttered in many ways: through songs and dance, chanted or narrated in rhetorical fashion, or simply uttered, and all with the right kinds of performative theatrics, such as affected vocalisations, evocative chants, and physical gestures. The performance requires no mimesis but performers may have recourse to it if they think imitation enhances their message and drives home their point.

Starting in the community square, the performers move from place to place, seeking out verbal combatants on their way home or to other parts of the community where the abuses are repeated. Presentations never remain the same—they are often varied to suit the new context of interaction, a necessity if performers are to retain their following. This goes on everywhere in the community where women and girls are willing to join in the abuse, culminating in the climactic act on the fourth day. The climactic act is performed by a cast of women worshippers of *Ezealaelu* (carriers) whose actions are designed to cleanse the community of the curses and abuses released by individuals during the previous three days.

Scope and Context as Pre-requisites for Performance: Sites and Locales

It is difficult to speak of space use in the presentations described above without considering the different sites and locales where they were staged. Charles Gore's analysis reveals how difficult it is to identify any one performance site or location as more important than the other, or as the performance space. Both performances negotiate communal landscapes and universes and use the staged events at different locales to reclaim (in Benin) and to heal (in Ochii, Ogwa) community. The universe they deal with is simultaneously metaphysical and material and the actions at the various sites generally direct attention to that universe at a macro level. The recourse to familiar sites and locations of social and ritual significance is important in how people make meaning of the presentations. In *Ohen*, the actions at the personal shrines and public places signal Benin ritual continuity, cultural homogeneity, and identity in the face of huge social changes that threaten the society. The *Ako Otuo* presentation is therapeutic and purges the Ochii section of Ogwa community.

The performers' link with the physical terrain is important to both presentations and, in the case of the *Ohen* of Benin, Gore suggests that:

> [A] separation of ritual and performance denies local means of conceptualization of agencies in the spirit world that intervene in the material world, which engenders the performative constituent of ritual. (1998: 78)

Gore's integrated universe applies to the *Ako Otuo* festival; however, the fact that *Ako Otuo*, *Ohen*, and similar performances in Africa are designed to reiterate and celebrate cosmic unity and to redress breaches in the metaphysical-material continuum through ritual displays and fictional dramatisations that reflect a community's universe suggests—as well as highlights—a spatial construct different from contemporary performance in its concept and use.

A significant difference between the two forms is that although contemporary performances focus on human conditions and histories, they operate in a different universe and do not necessarily seek to retain the integrated metaphysical-material world of indigenous communities. The difference is quite clear—even in modern plays based on myths, legends, and histories, such as Osofisan's *Morountodun* (1982), *Another Raft* (1988), and *Many Colours Make the Thunder-King* (1997)—the spatial construct is one of rationalism or that which calls for the objective separation of belief and faith from historical and material realities. The result, contrary to the condition in indigenous communities, is a universe that privileges the material world over the metaphysical, and a spatial relation that advocates their separation.

In indigenous performance settings, space may be related to locale but it has nothing to do with locating all the objects of a performance in a single spot or designated locale, as we have in many modern performances in which all stage action is placed before the audience. Here we are referring to an aesthetic convention in which space is a meeting-point, a place for all manners of participatory interactions involving different people in various activities ranging from participation in dance and music to ululations and chorus clapping. The context, purpose, and scope of a good number of indigenous performances influence how sites and locales in a community are deployed to spatial roles. Their meanings and outcomes depend on where they are staged, the significance of the locales themselves, the contents of presentations and their relationships to cultural fragments and artefacts outside the main presentation arenas. In effect, the main functions of spatial constructs, other than as spaces for staging performances, are to use places of performance to mirror and embody the contiguous relationship between the metaphysical and material worlds, to make the physical environment a truly meaningful part of this relationship and a factor in the presentation (Schechner, 1994).

The spatial relations described here produce what Marvin Carlson describes very elegantly as "ludic space" or "a permanently or temporarily created ludic space, a ground for the encounter of spectator and performer" (1989: 229–230). While such encounters are fictional and depend essentially on mimesis in contemporary performances, they function differently in indigenous performances. In the latter, people perform themselves *in situ* without being mimetic, and even though some members of a community may dissociate themselves from such sentiments, there are no distinctions between dramatic and socio-sacral worlds—the presentations are existential and real.

Kwabena Bame (1991) recounts C. M. Doke's (1936) account of the staging of the *Gemsbok* play of the Khomani people of Southern Africa, in which male performers dramatise and mimic the hunting of the gemsbok and depict "the killing of springbok by lions" (Bame, 1991: 51). In the course of the presentation, the play expands in scope as it incorporates other locales, gradually assimilating every object and person within its vicinity. Bame and Doke regard the Khomani universe as the setting for the drama in which the earth serves as the "stage" (Bame, 1991: 51). Doke describes the "earth stage", that Bame mentions here, as consisting of "the veld, trees, and grass" of the surrounding landscape where the plays are staged. According to Doke:

> each actor has his part and plays it in no unmistakable way. Old and young, male and female participate! Only the very aged being excluded owing to the strenuous nature of the acting in most cases. (Doke, 1936: 64–65; cited in Bame, 1991: 51)

A very short extract of Doke's description indicates the difficulty there is in attempting to limit the performance space, and how presentations that start on specific locales expand into a flexible, extended, indefinite space:

> … three or four hunters fully armed come out with a dozen or more boys… These later spread out among the tussocks of grass, running on hands… disappear over the dune, soon to appear just above where the gemsbok is resting… the gemsbok… makes off as fast as he can run for the nearest thorn bush… All the participants thoroughly enjoy this acting, though the one acting gemsbok sometimes complain that he gets more rough handling

and prodding with sticks than he cares for. (Doke, 1936: 466–467)

The scope of this presentation poses obvious spatial challenges. The performers' desire to re-enact the physical rigours of the chase and the gemsbok's almost human instinct for escape and survival will be lost in a confined space in which the actors (depicting the hunters, accompanying dogs, gemsbok, and human on-lookers) are constrained from exercising the very speed, guile, and fast-paced action that are required for a successful hunt. At the same time, it is difficult to identify with any certainty where the performance space begins and ends. The subsuming of extensive physical landscape and its constituent topographical features to the requirements of the presentation is more common than rare.

The spatial arrangement described here is not entirely pragmatic; it is neither designed to be logical nor dependent on what is available. Groups may select locations that offer the right kind of context or which facilitate the truthful, if not realistic depiction of events. Consequently, while strips of physical terrain, biological objects such as trees and anthills, and other set pieces may be ignored or be incorporated as actants (and perhaps prompting relativist questions about the relevance of set props that are not used in the presentation), performers are not averse to spatial disruptions and re-configurations that are essential for their presentations. Spatial construct in such settings has little to do with venue (which is often physically limiting), it is more precisely to do with representing and incorporating different sites and locales and their cultural associations as a means for embodying and reflecting the overarching meaning and purposes of presentations within a community.

Image, Symbol and Space

Visual imagery is important in many performance traditions. John Fletcher argues that:

> what we see on the stage affects us far more rapidly and directly than what we read on the page. The scenic space is a totality in which décor and props, costume and gesture impress us as an almost simultaneous object. (1982: 13)

It is the nature of many non-realistic performances to deal largely in signs and symbols, and as Leonard Pronko has argued, the kinds of indigenous performances I am referring to here—whether in Africa, in Asia, in Europe, or in the Americas—are, rich in signs, never masking them beneath an illusion, but instead allowing us the double experience of actor *and* character which has been the theatrical experience since the beginning. (1982: 42)

Consequently, although conventional modern performances use "fixed decors masquerading as forests, battlefields, palaces, costumes with conventional colours to indicate character, race, function" (Pronko, 1982: 41), indigenous performances often combine the real and the symbolic so that performers and participants can encounter performances through theatrical signs, but, more significantly, in a space that is both real and "*concrete*" (Kirby and Kirby, 1971). Here I use concrete to imply that in indigenous performances people's experience of space may be aesthetic in certain respects, but it is also essentially cultural.

The concept of concrete experience was first proposed by Kirby and Kirby who used the term in their analysis of the "Variety Show Manifesto" to refer to the experience of something "for its own sake rather than for its references and implications…" and as something that "is 'there' rather than referring to something that is not there" (1971: 20–21). Indigenous performance space is functional and non-localised; it has more than an aesthetic relationship with the performance it hosts and depends on the status and on the socio-sacral purposes and roles that it serves in a society for its effect and meaning.

The relationship between space and performance is real, not artificial and make-believe as in contemporary modern performance, in which space is essentially aesthetic and has little existential relationship with the presentation it hosts, in the way that the set of Chekhov's *The Cherry Orchard* will never be anything other than a theatrical appurtenance for the actors. For participants at indigenous performances, space incorporates the physical and metaphysical milieus and the two co-exist even within the ephemerality of the performance moment. This ensures that the cultural and, in some cases, the ritual status of performance spaces are factored in the creative process as well as in the production and reception strategies. For indigenous performances, this in effect, "maximizes the sensory dimensions and minimizes or eliminates the intellectual aspects" (Kirby and Kirby, 1971: 21) associated with space use and spatial relationships in modern contemporary performances.

Symbols and signs dominate performances and are most often enhanced through visual images. At their most elaborate, visual images generate colourful spectacle and make it possible for people to observe as well as participate in performances some distance away from the staging arena. *Ijele* performance in Igbo-speaking states of Nigeria—and in fact, most of West African masking—does not, as a matter of aesthetic principle, require audiences and participants in close proximity to the action. Some indigenous performances take their acts to anywhere they want and stage their actions in specified and non-specified locations throughout the community. Others may be localised to specific spots, yet the presence in the community of temporal activities and celebrations that reference them in other places across the community extend their supposed spaces.

In some itinerant displays it is not uncommon to have stationery stages or elements. Where they exist, these stages may be only one aspect of presentations that actively encourage the mobility of performers and participants and the incorporation of objects, locations, and thoroughfares between active moments in the course of presentations. The function of design in the indigenous performances referred to in this chapter is to make all the visual images accessible to people wherever they may be within reasonable distances from the main presentation places. In place of elaborate details there is usually symbolic representation, while abstraction that is sufficiently suggestive of the intended idea without confusing participants is preferred over realism. The level to which visual images and symbols affect space design and use in indigenous performances strung over large areas and locales has received little attention from performance theorists; this ought to be investigated to distinguish it from space use in contemporary performances.

Spatial Arrangements: Space as Site, Venue as Locale

Schechner's argument for "the exchange of space" in which "spectators become 'scene-makers as well as scene-watchers'" (1994: xxvi) brings me to some fundamental questions from which I propose a different way of looking at the concept of space in indigenous performance contexts in Africa. "Where do performance spaces begin and end in indigenous performances?" Is performance space merely a matter of the relationship between performers and participants, and is it determined by the spatial separation of performers from their audiences? Does it begin or end with participants who are free to participate wherever they choose, such as is the case in mask chases when participants taunt masks to chase them far away from main staging locales? Does this type of spatial relationship call for a re-thinking of how we analyse space in indigenous African performances? Do current critical parameters and languages such as space and venue reflect spatial praxis in indigenous performances?

The answers to these questions suggest a re-thinking of space and reception discourses. In the first place, some practitioners—notably Artaud (1964; repr. 1993), Appia, Beacham (1993), Craig (cited in Walton, 1983), and Brook (1972) had in the past tried to redefine spatial relations and audience reception in conventional theatres. All three drew ideas and paradigms from indigenous performances without necessarily highlighting why and how the contexts, purposes, and scopes of modern performances distinguish and distance them from indigenous counterparts with which they share aesthetic principles. The distinctiveness of spatial constructs, presentation contexts, the place of belief worlds and cosmos, and reception strategies in the two forms are yet to receive proper critical scrutiny beyond generalisations. These constitute some of the reasons why performance discourse continues to apply the modern principles of space use to indigenous performances. Out of the modern performance practitioners and critics, Brook, Schechner, Chaudhuri, Pearson, and Shanks have come closest to distinguishing between site and space, and locale and venue, but—like many other theorists—they stop short of proposing site and locale as more appropriate critical terms and alternative aesthetic definitions for space and venue in the interrogation of indigenous open air, environmental performances.

There are six main reasons why I think that the modern notion of space is problematic when applied to indigenous performances in Africa. First and foremost is the fact that when compared with site and locale, space (although connoting limitless expanse) conveys a sense of formulaic, structured form, fixed spatial boundaries, and the assumption that audiences require total visibility of every area of the stage and the actions in it. Indigenous performances, itinerant and open air, are not averse to these basic requirements, but the questions posed by Peter Brook in *The Empty Space* (1972)—about the simplicity and elasticity of staging spaces, whether the design of performance stages and theatre buildings ought to be based on the exactness of dimensions and symmetry, or on asymmetry and disorder—are still as valid today as they were when contemporary African performances emerged partially from, in reaction, and beside their indigenous counterpart. The fact is that since indigenous performances grew out of the need to deploy theatre to the task of restoring socio-sacral harmony, it is only logical to expect the form and its spatial arrangements to replicate, reflect, and embrace—in some physical sense—something of the existential contours of universes they address, as well as integrate their metaphysical and material features in presentations.

My second reason is that space reflects the kind of structured arrangement, order and symmetry, and fixed boundaries that indigenous performance aesthetics disrupt and do not conform to. Although some kind of formulaic order is a cherished feature of all performances everywhere, categorical rigidity of any sort is alien to the cosmology and universe of many indigenous African societies. Conceptually, space construct and use in indigenous African performance are at best asymmetrical, to borrow Brook's (1972) phrase. Such spaces are not only multifarious and flexible in use, they are generally large and diverse, consisting of and embracing part of the natural topography rather than being constructed upon the landscape. As in the examples discussed in this chapter, their designs embrace semantic disorder because the universe they frame is often characterised by dislocations, breaches, and tenuous relationships that a majority of the performances, especially rituals, seek to accommodate and resolve. In the societies under discussion, there are no categorical divisions between material and metaphysical worlds or binary distinctions between the living and dead, symbolic and literal. For these reasons, spatial designs do not aim to distance or distinguish performance from reality—their purpose is not to sanitise or deny socio-sacral objects, locations, and sites of any of their cultural significance, but rather to reinforce them as equal and essential ingredients in the performance or celebration of *communitas*.

My third reason is that the cultural status that some sites and locations enjoy makes it mandatory for their incorporation and the integration of their special literal and ritual meanings in indigenous performances. Because of the cultural function and status of such locales and sites, the uses to which their constituent actants—such as shrines and ritual objects—are deployed in the course of presentations, the contents of such displays, and the materiality of the performance moment communicate information about the performers and their societies. Sometimes symbolism is all that performers and participants require for interaction with each other within and beyond particular locations. The places used for indigenous performances, such as the three analysed above (*Ohen*, *Ako Otuo*, and Gemsbok play) are far more significant in terms of the extent to which they and the contents of a performance reflect and reinforce their respective community's universe. This is the primary reason why the concept and use of space in such performances is, essentially speaking, more archaeological (Pearson and Shanks, 2001) and performative than theatrical, and why both ought to be viewed differently from their counterparts in contemporary fictional performance.

My fourth reason is that visibility, whether total or partial, is a feature of performance presentation and reception. Visibility is a logical aspect of spatial constructs and relations that operates differently in indigenous performances. Una Chaudhuri offers a compelling critique in which she problematises spatial dynamics in the theatre as a *"geopathology"* (2000: xii) that derived from:

> the stage practice of early modern drama, specifically by the spatial arrangements of naturalism, which function according to a logic of *total visibility*. (2000: xii)

Chaudhuri points out that different staging practices and approaches—from expressionism to symbolism, absurdism, and epic theatre, to mention a few—have since encouraged the re-thinking and rejection of this early model of space use. Despite this, the requirement for visibility, even if this is only partial, and the proximity of audiences to props and set properties within well-defined spatial zones is still a prevalent feature of modern performance practices and criticism.

Visibility of the stage action and the proximity of audiences to the stage remains a central element of many performance forms, including those like happenings, installations, and site-specific pieces that resist the usual stage-audience dynamic or the separation of stage and auditorium. Indigenous performance spaces, as Chaudhuri argues, are less about visibility than they are about people celebrating their community in places and locales with authentic archaeological and socio-cultural referents to the performers and participants' universe. Spatial analysis, in the form, ought to be about participation and the extent to which performers and participants can do the required performance business from any vantage point without necessarily being in the same site and locale or in direct proximity to a stage, or even participating in all stages and features of a presentation. In other words—and this is very important—because there is neither the need nor the logic in such performances for an architectural structure that houses a special presentation spot as well as accommodating performers and audiences/participants, the application of contemporary performance aesthetics to the types of indigenous performances discussed above is both moot and irrelevant.

My fifth reason is the context and scope of indigenous performances. Elsewhere (Ukaegbu, 2007), I describe indigenous African performances such as masking and festivals that attract large numbers of masks and performers as a form of total theatre that—although different from the Western concepts that developed through Barrault, Artaud, Dullin, Copeau, Craig, and Appia—still captures the essence of what Christopher Innes describes as "total spectacle", in which the aim is to create a "theatrical stage world" that is "more expressive than reality" (Innes, 1984: 118). Innes's proposal favours theatre over the depiction of socio-cultural reality and *communitas*, and refers to modern western performance aesthetics.

Beside and different from Innes is Mineke Schipper's (1982) total theatre in Africa, a form in which the depiction of socio-cultural universe is as important as art and theatricality. African total theatre, of which many indigenous forms can be cited as good examples, could be simultaneously epic in magnitude and specific enough to incorporate or draw its contents from myths and legends, ancestral tales, genealogies, and folktales. It draws its component art forms from music, song and dance, storytelling and rituals, puppetry, and masquerading; it may include tragedies, comedies, and farce without necessarily distinguishing between comic and tragic genres; and may involve both anthropomorphic and theriomorphic characters in one performance space.

Indigenous performances, such as *Ijele*, that involve diverse art forms of music and dancing, huge spectacle and extensive participation spread over localised and non-localised spaces are unimaginable in confined spaces. Their extensive stage businesses disrupt conventional definitions for venue. The fact that *Ijele* presentations and the like deal with the universe of the people for whom they are created requires that as a matter of necessity, they represent this universe in its totality—encapsulating the realistic and illusionary, and the permanent and the temporary. In *Ijele*, the performer's body, make-up, and costuming are sites of representation. Everything from the context of presentations, props, stage business, and how space is used are there to serve the performance and the invisible other(s) whose presence is essential and in some instances, the primary reason for the performances. Pearson and Shanks describe the features and components of such performances as:

> the ecology of performance—that matrix of environment, people, and events and the narratives generated – which may represent its basic descriptive and analytical unit. (2001: 54)

My contention here is that the scope and context of *Ijele*, and the other presentations described in this chapter, entail more than a lot of movements from performer and participants. They demand the incorporation of essential parts of the physical landscape into performances, instead of merely representing them. Such an extensive "ecology of performance" (Pearson and Shanks, 2001) is difficult to achieve and sustain, if not impossible in enclosed spaces. What indigenous performances require and emphasise is a "spatial give-and-take as well as the full use of a spatial domain that continually modulates its boundaries" (Schechner, 1994: xxviii), as is the case in the examples cited in this chapter.

My sixth and final reason is that indigenous performance sites and locales are neither fixed nor can they be determined by geometry. There may be indefinite ways in how spaces and locales may be used, however, that is not to imply that they are boundless. Far from that, because although performers and participants "do not stand still" in a given locale or site, they range across them "over a defined territory" (Schechner, 1994: xxviii), defined by historical and cultural geographies. As Schechner argues:

> the space of the performance is defined organically by the action. Spectators watch from a variety of perspectives, some paying close attention, some ignoring the goings-on. (1994: xxviii)

In effect, while it is the responsibility of performers to maintain performance limits, this is a role they undertake with participants. The performance behaviour of either party has the potential to de-stabilise notions of a fixed space and the nature of the stage-audience relationship. For example, actions such as paying close attention or ignoring for the purpose of infuriating and taunting an aggressive mask into a chase is usually the prescribed performance behaviours and recipe for extending performances, as in a good number of African mask performances. Such behaviours do not only allow participants to become, in Schechner's words, the "scene-makers and scene-watchers", the spatial boundaries shift with actions to wherever participants are or invite performance business. The spatial dynamic described here is one of the unique defining features of indigenous African performances, in the sense that while the movement of audiences outside a theatre building would impact on meaning and reception in modern performances, this neither affects reception experience nor impairs meaning in indigenous presentations.

Conclusion

Indigenous performance space is not about seeing everything in one place, it is about participants shifting position and going along with the action to wherever the show moves. This spatial arrangement is not only about space use, it includes how culturally and ritually significant sites—for instance, shrines and ecological features such as trees and rivers and objects—across a community's topography are factored into and are part of performances. The modern theatre's search for "the ideal of an intense, common experience" (Chaudhuri, 2000) for performers and audiences is what indigenous performances have always had by way of spatial relationships. This raises the question as to whether Artaud's (1964; repr. 1993) vision of abolishing the conventional bifurcation of stage-auditorium and its replacement with a single site has been realised or thwarted by modern performances.

Artaud's suggestion for the eradication of spatial boundaries between stage and auditorium by placing the audience in the middle and heart of the action was more than a mere exercise in space dynamics—this is an objective that indigenous African performances have always achieved, and an acknowledgement of the obvious differences in comparison with the western-derived spatial conventions that Brook and Schechner have sought to address in one way or another. A spatial code that primarily views performance spaces as venues and structures to which people are drawn in order to enhance their aesthetic involvement and identification with a performance is at odds in indigenous performance presentation and reception strategies.

In different ways, Artaud, Brook, Schechner, Chaudhuri, Pearson, and Shanks highlight the distinctions and uniqueness of each of the indigenous African and West European spatial conventions. Of them all, Schechner—rather than Artaud or Brook—comes closest, in his search for a poetics of site and locale in "Six Axioms for Environmental Theatre", to the indigenous space construct described here, in his suggestion in Axiom 2 that "all the space is used for performance" (Schechner, 1994: xxviii) and that "often the entire space is performing space—no one is 'just watching'" (1994: xxix). Even then, Schechner's proposed poetics falls short of the indigenous concept of space with respect to contemporary performance's emphasis on place as location for watching. This differs from the approach in indigenous African performances in which space and locale have always been more than an aesthetic frame for stage action.

Locale, space and the performer-participant dynamic in indigenous African performances may be factors in where and how performances are presented and received, but more importantly, they serve the function of reflecting a community's cosmos, a condition that demands nothing short of using the ecology, archaeology, biological, socio-cultural, metaphysical, and material topographies of the performing community in performing and reinforcing its universe. Thus locale, space and their related performer-participant dynamic are intrinsic, concrete (Kirby and Kirby, 1971) elements of the contents, contexts, production, and reception of presentations. It is for these reasons that this chapter suggests that in place of space and venue, performance discourse ought to distinguish spatial relationships in indigenous African performances by substituting the two terms with sites and locales.

References

Artaud, A. (1964 repr.1993) *The Theatre and its Double*. Trans. Victor Corti (first published in Great Britain 1970). London: Calder.

Balme, C. (1999) *Decolonizing the Stage: Theatrical Syncretism and Post-Colonial Drama*. Oxford: Oxford University Press.

Bame, K. N. (1991) *Profiles in African Traditional Popular Culture Consensus and Conflict: Dance, Drama, Festivals and Funerals*, New York: Clear Type Press Inc.

Beacham, R. C. ed. (1993) *Texts on Theatre/Adolphe Appia*. London: Routledge.

Bharucha, R. (1993) *Theatre and the World: Performance and the Politics of Culture*. London and New York: Routledge.

Brook, P. (1972) *The Empty Space*. Harmondsworth: Penguin.

Carlson, M. (1989) *Places of Performance: The Semiotics of Theatre Architecture*. Ithaca: Cornell University Press.

Chaudhuri, U. (2000) *Staging Places: The Geography of Modern Drama*. Ann Arbor: The University of Michigan Press.

Cohen-Cruz, J., Schutzman, M. eds. (2006) *A Boal Companion: Dialogues on Theatre and Cultural Politics*. New York, London: Routledge.

Cresswell, T. (1997) "Imagining the Nomad: Mobility and the Postmodern Primitive." *Space and Social Theory: Interpreting Modernity and Postmodernity*. Ed. G. Benko and U. Strohmeyer. Oxford: Blackwell. pp. 360 –379.

Doke, C. M. (1936) "Games, Plays and Dances of the Khomani Bushmen." *Bantu Studies* 10: pp. 466–471.

Gore, C. (1998) "Ritual, Performance and Media in Urban Contemporary Shrine Configurations in Benin City in Nigeria." *Ritual, Performance, Media. ASA Monograph 35*. Ed. Felicia Hughes-Freeland. London and New York: Routledge. pp. 66–84.

Fletcher, J. (1982) "Symbolic Functions in Dramatic Performance." *Themes in Drama 4: Drama and Symbolism*. Ed. James Redmond. Cambridge: Cambridge University Press. pp. 13–28.

Hilton, J. (1987) *Performance*. Basingstoke: Macmillan [New Directions in Theatre].

Innes, C. (1984) *Holy Theatre: Ritual and the Avant Garde*. Cambridge and London: Cambridge University Press.

Kirby, M. and Kirby, V. N. (1971) *Futurist Performance*. New York: PAJ Publications.

Okagbue, O. A. (1987) "Theatre on the Street: Two Nigerian Samples." *Maske Und Kothurn: Internationale Beitrage*, 33 JAHRGANG. pp. 159–164.

Okagbue, O. (2007) *African Theatres and Performances.* London and New York: Routledge.

Osofisan, F. (1982) *Morountodun and Other Plays.* Lagos: Longman.

—. (1988) *Another Raft.* Lagos: Malthouse Press.

—. (1997) "Many Colours Make the Thunder-King" in *Major Plays 1* (2000). Ibadan: Opon Ifa Readers.

Pavis, P. (1992) *Theatre at the Crossroads of Culture.* Trans. Loren Kruger. London: Routledge.

—. (1996) "Towards a Theory of Interculturalism in Theatre?" *The Intercultural Performance Reader.* Ed. Patrice Pavis, London: Routledge. pp. 1–21

Pearson, M. and Shanks, M. (2001) *Theatre/Archaeology.* London and New York: Routledge.

Pronko, L. C. (1982) *"Kabuki:* Signs, Symbols and the Hieroglyphic Actor." *Themes in Drama 4: Drama and Symbolism.* Ed. James Redmond. Cambridge: Cambridge University Press. pp. 42–55.

Schechner, R. (1994) *Environmental Theatre.* New York and London: Applause.

Schipper, M. (1982) *Theatre and Society in Africa.* Johannesburg: Ravan Press.

Soyinka, W. (1988) *Art, Dialogue and Outrage: Essays on Literature and Culture.* Ibadan: New Horn Press.

Turner, V. (1974) *Drama, Fields and Metaphors: Symbolic Action in Human Society.* Ithaca: Cornell University Press.

Ukaegbu, V. (2004) "Performing Postcolonially: Contextual Changes in the Adaptations of Wole Soyinka's *Death and the King's Horseman* and Femi Osofisan's *Once Upon Four Robbers." World Literature Written in English.* 40(1); (2002–03): pp. 71–85.

—. (2007) *The Use of Masks in Igbo Theatre in Nigeria: The Aesthetic Flexibility of Performance Traditions.* Lewiston, New York, and Lampeter: Edwin Mellen Press.

Walton, M. J. ed. (1983) *Craig on Theatre.* London: Methuen.

Wolford, L. and Shechner, R. eds. (2001) *The Grotowski Sourcebook.* London: Routledge.

CHAPTER THREE

DREAMS DEFERRED:
NATIONAL THEATRES AND NATIONAL
DEVELOPMENT IN AFRICA

OSITA OKAGBUE

Introduction

At the core of this chapter is a strong conviction that it is mainly in the realm of culture that African nations can compete effectively with the rest of the world, including the so-called "developed" nations of the West. Unfortunately, however, this cultural domain—where the playing field is naturally unbiased and thus relatively level, and where, in some instances, Africa may actually have a comparative advantage—appears to be the least of the worries of African leaders and policy-makers who have consistently conceived of progress and development as being just the borrowing of Western technology, models of education, and systems of social, economic, and political organisation. Chinua Achebe's trenchant opening sentence in his book, *The Trouble with Nigeria* (1983), that the "trouble with Nigeria is simply and squarely a failure of leadership" remains true to date—and he may as well be writing about African leaders as a whole.

It seems to me that the crop of leaders that have continued to emerge in different African nations since independence truly represent what Octave Mannoni had in mind when he put forward his infamous theory of the "dependency complex" of colonised peoples in *Prospero and Caliban: The Psychology of Colonization* (1950, 1990). Mannoni also advocates, as corollary to the dependency complex, the idea of an inferiority complex of the coloniser. Mannoni's theory ascribes peculiar psychological predispositions to both the colonised and the coloniser, which a colonial encounter/situation addresses and satisfies to the contentment of both. My argument here, therefore—and which subsequent readings of Mannoni have shown—is that he attempts in a classic colonialist (orientalist, à la Said) fashion to explain away the colonial situation as merely a matter of difference in psychologies, instead of one in which the rich dominate the poor, and the strong and powerful dominate the weak and powerless—a situation which consists of a systematic exploitation of difference in the apportionment of the standards of living.

In effect, Mannoni explains away what was, essentially, an economic and political situation as a mutually beneficial encounter between the psychologically needy colonised and an enterprising coloniser—both of whose unique complexes are satisfied by the colonial situation. However, one key question that remains is whether or not African leaders—since independence from colonialism and up to the present day—are unwittingly reinforcing Mannoni's colonialist argument and typology by their selfish and myopic continuation of the continent's social and economic stagnation, and by their stubborn refusal or inability to go beyond "dependence" on the West.

The condition of African dependence was, in the view of this essay, created by and during colonialism, and exists neo-colonially today as a way of ensuring that the coloniser surreptitiously maintains a continued dominance and interference in the lives of the colonised. Sadly for African states, the tragedy—as Achebe (1983) surmises—is Africa being bedevilled by a selfish, myopic and incompetent leadership that is riddled through and through by a politics and culture of dependence, and who have failed to live up to the responsibilities of their offices. These leaders, it appears, are afraid of Africa succeeding, afraid of their respective countries breaking away from their continued reliance on foreign solutions to local problems—they are reluctant to see Africa looking inwards in order to find out what her strengths and weaknesses are, and then basing programmes of solutions on maximising those strengths while diminishing the weaknesses.

That inward look will involve each African nation taking stock of its cultural base to discover what is already there and what is not, what works and what needs fixing. Unfortunately, this is not being done because it is almost as if these leaders are ashamed of their African cultures, and so they neglect their development and support, and they fail to see the central role that culture can play in national development. This chapter will return to this theme and the idea of cultural capital later on.

Culture, Colonialism and African Underdevelopment: Beyond the "Dependency Complex"

It is naïve to see Europe's imperial enterprise in Africa as a purely economic venture, just as it is simplistic to view colonialism as a mere military adventure by European nations motivated by a desire to conquer and dominate other peoples and lands. The civilising mission, so often put forward as justification for colonialism, can be easily dismissed outright for the great lie that it was. However, as well as being economic and military, colonialism was—at a much deeper level—a cultural project which was very destructive for colonised peoples. Military and economic conquest may have succeeded in subduing and enslaving colonised peoples, but the cultural conquest was the single most important factor that helped to make colonial domination stable and enduring, as the current neo-colonial relationship between erstwhile colonisers and colonised demonstrate. In fact, colonialism required cultural domination in order to entrench and sustain itself. The reason for the potency of the cultural dimension of colonialism is not difficult to deduce, because of the centrality of culture in peoples' lives and existence.

Culture is the mainstay of a people—it provides a group with the mechanisms and instruments for dealing with life and with their environment. If this is challenged, if this basis of a people's existence is undermined or marginalised—as it was under colonialism—then the core of the people's world is truly struck and wounded. According to Amilcar Cabral, to dominate a people, you do not need to fire a gun if you are able to destroy the people's culture. Cabral goes on to elaborate on this when he says that:

> History teaches us that, in certain circumstances, it is quite easy for a stranger to impose his rule on a people. But history equally teaches us that, whatever the material aspect to that rule, it cannot be sustained except by the permanent and organized repression of the cultural life of the people in question... For as long as a section of the populace is able to have a cultural life, foreign domination cannot be sure of its perpetuation. (1974: 12)

Certain questions inevitably arise from this. The first is: were African peoples deprived of their cultures against their wills by colonialism? The answer is: yes, but maybe not in all cases. The second question is: did colonialism succeed in putting a wedge between colonised Africans and their cultures? The answer is that it certainly did in many instances. It can be argued that the colonial enterprise impacted the indigenous cultures of the colonised in two ways: first, by interfering with and ultimately altering the course of African histories; and second, through introducing education systems that privileged Western modes of thought while concertedly denigrating African cultures, philosophies, and knowledge systems. It is thus obvious that cultural estrangement and disenfranchisement was a key colonial strategy to achieve total domination, both physical and mental— the latter often leading to what is referred to as the "colonial mentality syndrome" of the colonised.

In exploring the condition of colonial mentality in *Culture and Identity in African and Caribbean Theatre* (2009), I called to mind Albert Memmi's powerful portrait of the colonised and the coloniser. Memmi concludes his portrait of the colonised by saying that:

> The colonizer lives on for a very long time in the decolonized man and we will have to wait longer still before we see that really new man. (Memmi, 1965, and 1968: 188; cited in Okagbue, 2009: 25)

That the effects of colonialism remain with the colonised is evident and, in my view, is responsible for the lack of progress on many fronts, which has been the case with many African states. Formerly colonised African nation states may have achieved nominal political independence, but which of them have in reality achieved cultural and economic independence? Cabral, in his 1970 homage lecture to Eduardo Mondlane—the assassinated president of the Mozambican Liberation Front (FRELIMO) —is right when he also asserts that:

> A nation which frees itself from foreign rule will only be culturally free if, without a complex and without underestimating the importance of positive contributions from the oppressors' culture and of other cultures, it recaptures the commanding heights of its own culture... (1974: 13)

Thus one has to ask whether African nations are truly free politically, considering they operate borrowed political and economic systems that are essentially built on, and sustained by, a culture of dependence. These political and economic systems ensure that African governments and peoples are never in true control of their destinies, rather they are mere appendages or eternal peripheries in a world order that is still for, and controlled from, the metropolitan centres of the former colonisers. One of the key ingredients missing from the systems of governance, economic activities, and social practices (including education) in most African countries is the continued absence or deliberate marginalisation of African cultures and indigenous knowledge systems from the respective national policy frameworks.

An ancillary argument being put forward in this chapter, which will help to foreground the undeniably significant role that national culture(s) should play in a nation's development, is that indigenous cultures should be repositioned so they are at the heart of African development initiatives and strategies. These strategies should be designed to take on board the diversities and creative potentials of African cultures. If Africa's current underdevelopment or mis-development was achieved and maintained through the cultural actions of the colonisers and the continued cultural inactions or mis-actions of African governments, then the elimination of the continent's underdevelopment can only come about through the counter-cultural actions of African peoples.

The starting point of this remedial action must be with the elimination of the culture and politics of dependence on foreign aid, which characterises the relations between Africa and the rest of the economically developed world. Africa needs to first reconnect with its cultural base by understanding and updating its local knowledge systems and making them the bedrock of development policy initiatives and strategies, while remaining open to beneficial influences from elsewhere. The arts and arts institutions, such as the national theatre and cultural centres, have a central role to play in this, and the rest of this chapter will demonstrate how the national theatre can contribute to the process of reconnecting with, and repositioning of, African cultures in the project of moving beyond dependence.

Theatre, Culture and Identity

"By their performances shall ye know them", claims Victor Turner (1980). Turner goes on to elaborate on this idea when he asserts that:

> Cultures are most fully expressed in and made conscious of themselves in their ritual and theatrical performances. [...] A performance is a dialectic of "flow"... in which the central meanings, values and goals of a culture are seen "in action" as they shape and explain behaviour. A performance is declarative of our shared humanity, yet it utters the uniqueness of particular cultures. (Turner, 1980, cited in Schechner and Appel, 1990: 1)

Turner, here, hints at the complex interconnectedness of the relationship between theatre, culture, and identity. It is evident from this that a nation's theatre and performance practices provide unique opportunities and contexts for the nation and its peoples to engage in creative dialogue and discourse with their culture(s). In *Performing America: Cultural Nationalism in American Theater*, Mason and Gainor assert that in:

> the performative arena, in the interchanges among artists and spectators, we can enact narratives of nation, whether ostensibly actual or openly speculative. (1999: 1)

Equally, I argue elsewhere that:

> What theatres and performances do is appropriate new experiences, re-present them, and thereby in the process acting simultaneously as social memories and refractive indexes of their respective communities. Each performance is in dialogue with history, affecting and changing history as much as it is affected and changed by history. (Okagbue, 2007: 13)

There is thus, suggested in all the above, a dialectical relationship between any work of art and its social and cultural context, and this occurs as a "series of mediations and counter-mediations between art, culture and society" (Okagbue, 2007: 12) in which the three engage with, modify, and are ultimately modified by one another.

Each theatrical piece, as Maria Shevtsova (1993: ix) concludes, "no matter where it is constructed… vibrates with the movements of its society". Benedict Anderson's notion of imagined communities and the persuasive non-essentialist argument about identity imply that the very idea of nation or identity is inherently performative and that a culture is constantly "constructing and representing itself to itself as well as to others" (see Rosemarie Bank in Mason and Gainor, 1999: 9). Put another way, the nation—like any other identity—comes into being at the moment when it is performed and exists because it is performed, and the theatre is the central arena in which these enactments of the nation take place.

As a consequence of the preceding arguments, therefore, one can begin to appreciate the crucial role that a national theatre can play in the unearthing, management, dissemination, and preservation of the cultures and the inherent identity(ies) of a nation. But, are the national theatres in Africa living up to their responsibilities? To examine this, this chapter will look at the national theatres of Nigeria, South Africa, Uganda, Senegal, and Ghana. While I acknowledge that there are many other national theatres in Africa, this chapter will concentrate on the five above because they are the ones that I am most familiar with.

National Theatres and Africa's Cultural Capital

The continent of Africa is undoubtedly blessed with an abundance of cultural wealth. Thus Africa's problem is not a lack of cultural or other natural resources—rather, the continent's problem, in my view, is the inability to positively manage the resources with which African nations have been endowed. And in terms of Africa's cultural wealth, a key question is how equipped conceptually and materially are the national theatres and other cultural institutions in Africa to be able to manage this inherent resource. What African countries need very much are institutions and instruments of government that are able to transform the continent's cultural resources into usable and beneficial cultural capital to help improve the lives of the peoples who own these resources. The African countries mentioned above, and a few many others besides, have national theatres, or at least physical structures that have been so designated. But are any of these national theatres fit for purpose, and which of them is performing the roles that a truly national theatre should perform?

A close look at any of the national theatres of these African countries will reveal immediately that the majority of them fall far short of what is expected of a national theatre. But if we are to look at countries from other parts of the world, the picture is remarkably different. Take the Czech Republic, for instance, which sees its National Theatre as "the embodiment of the will of the Czech nation for its national identity and independence". This is further reinforced by Bibiana Papp, who feels that:

> For Czech people, the National Theatre is one of the most important cultural institutions in Prague. Since its inception [1868–81] the theatre has played an important role in the development of the Czech language, Czech music and the dramatic arts. (2012)

Zoltan Imre in "Staging the Nation: Changing Concepts of a National Theatre in Europe" expands on this when he writes that:

> While in the eighteenth and nineteenth centuries the notion of a national theatre was regarded in most Western Europe as a means of promoting national—or even imperial—integration, in Eastern Europe, the debates about and later the realization of national theatres often took place within the context of and against oppressive imperiums. But in both parts of Europe the realization of a national theatre was utilized to represent a unified nation in a virtual way, its role being to maintain a single and fixed national identity and a homogenous and dominant national culture. (2008: 75)

The same can be said of the national theatres in Wales and Scotland, where the national theatre serve as instruments for reasserting Welsh and Scottish identities that have been under threat of marginalisation by and from an imposed English/British identity.

Of which of the national theatres in Africa can similar claims be made? African nations share, with these nations of Europe, forms and histories of colonial domination and oppression. However, these nations have used their cultural institutions such as the national theatres—as suggested by Cabral earlier—as one of the ways of freeing themselves from their oppressors, but African states have not been able to achieve similar outcomes. Instead, some African governments continue to alienate their indigenous cultures, and fail to conceive of the centrality of these indigenous cultures to their quest for development. And even when African governments establish such cultural institutions as a national theatre, there is not the understanding of the role that such an institution can play in the development and maintenance of a national identity.

This chapter argues, therefore, that the failure of national theatres in Africa to live up to responsibilities expected of them can be attributed to the manner and instruments of their founding. Some of them seem to have emerged by accident, with the result that their reason for coming into being appears not to have been properly thought out before they were established or built. Moreover, in some cases they are conceived and thought of, first and foremost, as prestigious buildings or venues for hosting performances and other entertainment events for local and visiting performing groups or companies. Nigeria's National Theatre at Iganmu, Lagos, is a case in point. The National Theatre began life as part of the infrastructure to support Nigeria's hosting of the 1977 Festival of Arts and Culture, FESTAC 77—so the theatre was first and foremost conceived as a "venue" and only became the National Theatre afterwards. This accident of origin, it seems to me, has dogged the National Theatre of Nigeria and its ability to perform the roles expected of a national theatre ever since, with the result that it has not contributed in any significant way to the development of theatre and performance in Nigeria. It did provide a prestigious venue for performances, films, and other events in its heyday, but sadly the building is in almost terminal disrepair, which is a reflection of how it is regarded by the government and the people who have been charged with running it since it was built.

Responding critically to the recent "low interest intervention fund" of two hundred million dollars ($200 million) to the entertainment industry by President Goodluck Jonathan, Tope Babayemi retorts in a 2011 interview with Akintayo Abodunrin:

The area that needs funding is the area that belongs to Mr President
himself, the federal ministry of culture and tourism, its parastatals and
institutions. You don't need to take a close look to see that things are not
well in that area. Infrastructure that was set up to host the world, during
FESTAC 77, all have been allowed to dilapidate. Look at the national
theatre, it has no recognisable programme. All that goes on there are non-
art events.

What should a properly functioning national theatre be expected to
accomplish? In order to explore this question, I will now confine my
discussion to the five national theatres selected: The National Theatre,
Iganmu, Lagos; The Department of Arts and Culture under which exists
the various "national theatres" in South Africa, such as the South African
State Theatre in Pretoria and the Market Theatre in Johannesburg; The
Daniel Sorano Theatre (The Grand National Theatre), Dakar, Senegal; The
Ghana National Theatre, Accra; and the Uganda National Cultural Centre
and National Theatre, Kampala.

The Department of Arts and Culture in South Africa/ The National Arts Council

South Africa has always had a history of arts and cultural institutions right
from the apartheid period with the performing arts councils, which have
since been replaced by the National Arts Council (NAC), the Playhouses,
and the Large Scale Performing Arts Ensembles. The Department of Arts
and Culture (DAC) is the ministry responsible for managing arts and
culture in South Africa. Under the DAC, there are three chief directorates:
Arts and Culture in Society; Arts, Social Development and Youth; and
National Language Service. Under the Arts and Culture in Society
Directorate, there are five sub-directorates, namely: Playhouses and
Festivals, Performing Arts Portfolio, Funding Bodies, 2010 Arts and
Culture Programme, and Community Arts Centres. Included in the
Playhouses and Festivals sub-directorate are: the Market Theatre in
Johannesburg; the Performing Arts Centre of the Free State (PACOFS);
the South African State Theatre in Pretoria (Tshwane); Artscape Theatre
Centre in Cape Town; Windybrow Arts in Johannesburg; and the
Playhouse Company in Durban.

The DAC, through the National Arts Council (the council was
established by an act of parliament in 1997 and is the national agency
charged with developing South Africa's creative industry through the
award of grants to groups and individuals in the creative cultural sector)
and its various directorates and sub-directorates, is primarily charged with

developing and promoting "arts and culture in South Africa" and with highlighting the role both can perform in social development. The sub-directorate with the Performing Arts Portfolio has the responsibility:

> to develop, promote, preserve and sustain South Africa's performing arts and provide strategic support to the Large Scale Performing Arts ensembles. (DAC 2006)

The sub-directorate of Playhouses and Festivals, on the other hand, "provides strategic support for the six playhouses and "develops guidelines for the implementation of festivals, nationally, provincially and locally" (DAC, 2006). Another major remit of the sub-directorate of Playhouses and Festivals is the development and implementation of overall "strategies for the performing arts sector" and the development of audiences for the performing arts sector, while supporting the playhouses and initiating the national festivals.

One already knows the huge and significant role the Market Theatre played as part of the cultural struggle that challenged and ultimately helped in defeating apartheid. Many of the well-known anti-apartheid theatre makers and activists—such as Athol Fugard, John Kani, Winston Ntshona, Barney Simon, Mannie Manim (founders of the Market Theatre), Mbogeni Ngema, Percy Mtwa etc.—had performed at or were part of the Market Theatre. Another of the playhouses is the South African State Theatre (SAST), a huge building complex in Church Street in Pretoria/Tshwane, with five theatres and a huge public square, which was opened in 1981 as a non-profit, government funded company. It is famous for lavish productions that have included overseas opera singers and ballet dancers gracing the huge main stage. The opening of the theatre complex was a milestone in South Africa's theatre history and marked the beginning of great things to come. The State Theatre in Pretoria today plays a leading role in the development of the performing arts, and is host to the colourful variety of entertainment found among the diverse cultures of South Africa.

As well as the State Theatre's use of lavish staging, there is also a permanent opera ensemble and chorus, a ballet company, a dance company, a drama company, and all other departments necessary to support a working theatre. The State Theatre continues to host a variety of international and national shows, as well as supporting local talents. However, the South African State Theatre is much more than just a complex of performance venues. Functioning as a receiving house, this unusual, stylish, centrally situated venue can accommodate almost any performance, function, or special event, and does so, on a regular basis. The theatre's vision is clear and the SAST is described as a:

> national flagship that facilitates the arts & entertainment and encourages diverse culture provision; we seek to play a unique and vital role in the cultural life of the Nation, the Province of Gauteng and the City of Tshwane. (SAST, 2011: 2)

SAST also has a very compelling mission statement which includes the mandate to:

> present the very best performing arts work from the local community, the province, the country and from around the world …to provide development opportunities for emerging arts practitioners to learn and perform within the context of our programmes… to provide audience development programmes… (SAST, 2011: 2)

It is obvious, therefore, that South Africa has an organised network of performing arts management and provision in the mould of what a national theatre should do, and that if all the visions and mission statements of the DAC, the playhouses, and the Large Performing Arts Ensembles are realised, the theatre—and by extension, arts and culture—would continue to play a major role in the development of South Africa.

The Uganda National Cultural Centre and the National Theatre

The Uganda National Cultural Centre (UNCC) and National Theatre in Kampala is a statutory government body established by an act of parliament on 8 October 1959. The Centre celebrated its fifty year anniversary in 2009 and is described in its vision statement as a:

> vibrant institution guided by unity in diversity, integrity and relevance to national development, nourishing, celebrating and promoting art and culture. (UNCC, n.d.)

The Centre's mission is "to set standards, build capacity and implement national policies that, preserve, promote and develop Uganda's art and culture". As with the DAC and the playhouses in South Africa, the UNCC and National Theatre in Kampala has a clearly stated mandate which is: to provide and establish theatres and cultural centres; encourage and develop cultural and artistic activities; and provide a home to societies, groups and organisations that deal in art and culture. The UNCC Act which set up the Centre also mandates it to do the following: preserve, promote and popularise Uganda's cultural heritage, locally and internationally; entertain and educate the public using theatre and film; and enhance and safeguard the quality and standard of the arts in the country. One cannot, however, ascertain to what extent these national objectives are being met by the UNCC and the National Theatre.

The Nigeria National Arts Theatre

The National Arts Theatre in Iganmu, Lagos is one of the uniquely iconic emblems of contemporary Nigeria. At its inception in the mid-1970s, it represented the mood of the nation, a nation on the move, a proud nation, and a beacon to the African continent and the black race. The National Arts Theatre is much more than a building or architectural masterpiece, but has been described as the soul of the arts in the country. However, because the National Arts Theatre came into existence more by accident than by design, it has not been able to go beyond being just a spectacular building and a good performance/events venue. This does not mean that this wonderful and spectacular building, that dominates the landscape as one drives across the bridges that lead into mainland Lagos, was not carefully planned and executed; rather, it seems to me that the idea of what a national theatre is meant to be or do had not featured in the planning process for the building in Iganmu.

Nigeria was to host the 1977 Festival of African Arts and Cultures (FESTAC 77) and so a centralised venue was needed where the majority of the activities, including the many performances and the colloquium, could be housed, and thus a structure that could accommodate all of these was conceived and put in place. It was also conceived more as a showpiece building that could reflect Nigeria's economic boom of the time, than as a house of the nation's arts and culture. Although, the idea for a National Arts Theatre was initiated by the then government of General Yakubu Gowon, the desire to host FESTAC 77 was the main catalyst for the birth of the building.

Concrete arrangements for its establishment started in 1973, when the Federal Government appointed a 29-member Theatre Consultative Committee (TCC) to advise on the concept and organisational structure of a theatre. The committee proposed the establishment of a national theatre which should also be the home of a national troupe. However, I remain unconvinced that the idea of a national theatre in the mould of South Africa's DAC or the UNCC in Uganda happened in the Nigerian case, since it has proved difficult to access the vision and mission statement under which the National Arts Theatre was founded and run since 1977. Even to date, the management team of the National Arts Theatre are very evasive when they are asked for their vision or mission statement documents. Given this state of the National Arts Theatre, how can one realistically expect this supposedly cultural institution to fulfil its manifest role and function of preserving and promoting the arts and culture of the country?

The National Theatre, Ghana

Theatre and the idea of the Ghanaian nation have always been closely linked since colonial times and this link continued after independence in 1957. The quest for a postcolonial cultural and political identity has pre-occupied various leaders and governments in Ghana since independence, beginning from Kwame Nkrumah, the country's first president and continuing through Jerry Rawlings in his military and civilian incarnations as president of the country, to the present post-military democratic government of John Dramani Mahama. This search for a post-independence identity has, as Steve Collins (2007) points out, "given voice and focus to the unique National Theatre Company and developed the style of *Abibgromma*".

Ghanaian leaders throughout the country's history seem to have recognised the importance of culture in helping to define and assert the idea and contours of the nation. The idea of a national theatre for Ghana originated, and was in synchrony, with the idea and process of Ghana's emergence from colonial rule, and thus in 1957:

> the same year that Ghana became a nation the foremost practitioners of theatre, inspired by a new wave of energy and freedom, came together to form the National Theatre Movement to "help forge the new nation's cultural identity" and create a theatrical form of "truly Ghanaian flavour, drawing on oral traditions of performance." (Collins, 2007)

One name that was instrumental in the development of a sense of a truly national theatre form and practice was Efua Sutherland, who in 1958 founded the Experimental Theatre Players. In 1961, her company was officially endorsed and renamed the Ghana Drama Studio, with Joe de Graft—well-known dramatist, actor, and teacher—as its first director. Sutherland saw theatre as a medium for reaching, as well as a context for engaging with, the greatest number of people possible and she also believed in using drama as a tool for education and social change. As a belated outcome of the National Theatre Movement, a National Theatre Company was established in 1983 as "a model repertory troupe to facilitate teaching, research and experimentation" and its mission was to "evolve the concept of an authentic African theatre which draws from both traditional and contemporary legacies" (Collins 2007). It is, therefore, fitting that in 1992, on the very site of the Ghana Drama Studio, President Rawlings inaugurated the National Theatre of Ghana. The building, it is claimed, was designed to resemble sails being caught by the wind and propelling the affluence of Ghanaian theatre out into the wider world; and like the other theatres in South Africa and Nigeria, it is impressive and compels attention.

The PNDC Law 259 (All Things Ghana, 2012), which established the national theatre, outlined the major objectives of the theatre to include the following:

1. To promote and develop the performing arts in Ghana
2. To formulate criteria and conditions to regulate performance by Ghanaian and international artistes and troupes
3. To establish theatres in such parts of the country as the Government of Ghana may deem fit
4. To develop and promote a strongly integrated national culture through the performing arts
5. To assist in formulating an effective export promotion programme of works in the performing arts produced in Ghana and
6. To engage in other functions as the Government of Ghana may assign it.

The law, under Article 7, provides that there will be three resident groups, namely: the National Symphony Orchestra, the National Dance Company, and the National Drama Company.

Going by the advertised activities and programmes of these companies, it may be argued that a truly national theatre exists in Ghana. However, I have my doubts and I am worried by the fact that in undertaking a responsibility as important as managing a national culture, Ghana has continued to rely on China for help—first for the initial funding for the building, and many years later for funds to renovate it. This is as disturbing as the fact that in 2001, the then Nigerian government under President Olusegun Obasanjo (ironically the same man who as military head of state oversaw the completion of the Nigerian National Arts Theatre) actually contemplated privatising and selling the National Arts Theatre to private capital. What the Ghanaian situation recalls is the very post-independence culture of dependence which I opened the chapter with, bearing in mind that international aid, very often, is accompanied by significant influence on the part of the aid donor, and the occasional mortgage of national principles and interests on the part of the recipient.

The Théâtre National Daniel Sorano, Dakar, Senegal

The first national theatre of Senegal is known as the Théâtre National Daniel Sorano (Daniel Sorano National Theatre), and it was the brainchild of the country's first president, Leopold Sedar Senghor. The theatre was opened in July 1965, and its name pays homage to the Franco-Senegalese actor/comedian, Daniel Sorano. The theatre was set up as its mission statement proclaims to research, publicise, and preserve the numerous performance traditions and practices of the country. Structurally, the theatre has three departments or companies: the Senegalese National Ballet, the National Drama Troupe of Senegal, and the Oral/Lyric Performing Group. Recently, a new theatre has been built to replace the Daniel Sorano. This new theatre, which is known as the Grand National Theatre, was built by the Chinese as a "gift" to Senegal, and was commissioned in 2009 by President Abdoulaye Wade. As was the case in Ghana and a number of resource-rich countries in the African continent, the Chinese appear to now have the knack of altruistically coming to the rescue of African national cultural institutions.

What has emerged from this cursory look at the national cultural institutions of the five African countries is that, with the exception of South Africa, the national theatres in Africa do not seem be fulfilling the very functions that are clearly stated in their vision and mission statements. For instance, none of the other four national theatres seem to have put in place strategies, structures, and programmes for researching, promoting, celebrating, preserving, and managing the arts and cultures of their respective countries. On paper, these national theatres state the ideals of a national theatre, but, from interviews and personal visits, the reality is that credible programmes are not actually put in place to support the achievement of these objectives. This inevitably leads one to wonder what the way forward is for Africa's failed or failing national theatres.

Rethinking National Theatres in Africa

There is no doubt that the idea of a national theatre—as we have seen in the five case studies above—is firmly anchored in, and intrinsically linked with, the evolution and articulation of the sense of nation in each case. The national theatre certifies, as it were, the emergence or existence of the nation. This need arises more often in contexts preceded by periods of political domination and oppression, as was the case with the African nations under European colonial rule. Four of the five case studies— Ghana, Nigeria, Senegal, and Uganda—went through fairly similar colonial experiences (Senegal though underwent assimilation, whereas Ghana and Nigeria, and to some extent Uganda, experienced indirect rule), and for all four, the idea of a national theatre was synonymous and evolved alongside the nationalist movements in each country. It seemed that in each case there was a realisation that the culture and arts of the colonised African country needed to be liberated from colonial domination and marginalisation, and that the national theatre was the institution to do this.   In the early days in Ghana, especially with the experimental work of Sutherland and de Graft, a genuine effort was made to recover and reposition indigenous Ghanaian performance practices and use these to fashion a national theatre form and practice. I am not aware of any such work in Nigeria, even though I know of Hubert Ogunde's attempt to evolve a form of national choreography in the 1970s and 1980s. However, this did not have the same strategic and sustained research oriented approach that Sutherland adopted. I cannot speak authoritatively about the precise work that was done to create a national theatre aesthetic in Senegal and Uganda. In South Africa, the white minority government also needed its own national theatre as a way of marking it out from its European ancestry, while facilitating the coming together of the various European cultures that had settled in the country.

As pointed out at the beginning of this chapter, culture played a significant role in the European colonial domination of Africa, and we have also seen that culture also played a crucial part in the nationalist anti-colonial/decolonisation movements across the continent (although this was sometimes on a very superficial and Machiavellian level). Consequently, as part of reclaiming their cultural heritages, which had either been marginalised or in some cases severely immobilised by the colonial powers, the nationalists movements and the subsequent new nations that emerged after independence had to reclaim, recuperate, and reassert their indigenous cultures as part of that process of articulating and asserting their emerging identities as newly independent nations. Thus, a concrete symbol of this reclamation was the establishment of national theatres or forms of national cultural centres. It is unfortunate, however, that this very important component of the drive for independence and a new national identity has not been realised, hence the title of the chapter.

The phenomenon of postcolonial and post-independent reclamation of indigenous cultures, one must point out, is not peculiar to Africa. Indeed, the same thing has happened in other parts of the world, particularly in contexts in which nations have been previously colonised or politically dominated. One of the first things nations or cultures do is reclaim a lost, marginalised, or traumatised indigenous/autochthonous identity, which a colonising power would very often attack or seriously undermine as part of its strategy of domination. Political independence brings with it a sense of being a nation and a pre-domination (pre-colonial) cultural heritage plays a huge part in cementing this new sense of nation, because this new nation has to seek ways to prove that it is different from the oppressor or coloniser. For African nations, however, this is even more complicated because colonialism had meant in many instances the yoking together of different pre-colonial nations and cultures into single national entities and political arrangements, and so a national theatre in the context of Africa has an even more fundamental role to play in melding the various cultures and peoples of each new nation by providing a shared national space and framework for these cultures to find and meet each other, and in the process to negotiate and articulate their shared sense of oneness.

The idea of a national theatre is in reality more complex and more deeply textured than it often appears, especially to some of the very individuals involved in or tasked with the responsibility of setting it up. There is a clear cultural politics which underpins or should underpin/inform the very idea of a national theatre, and the initiators and managers of Africa's national theatres must never lose sight of this, whether at the concept phase or in the subsequent daily affair of running such theatres.

There are principally three ways of looking at or understanding a national theatre:

1. National theatre as a political/cultural idea/concept.
2. National theatre as a building.
3. National theatre as an institution/organising framework.

First, as a political or cultural idea or concept, a national theatre is underpinned by a sense of nationalism and it is set up to address issues of nationhood, especially the nation's cultural identity. This is more so when the nation in question has faced, or is still facing, cultural and political imperialism. The national theatre within this frame of thought is responsible for or tasked with excavating, articulating, promoting, and preserving the national and cultural identities of the nation and its constituent peoples. In the second instance, the national theatre can be conceived of as a building—a national monument which houses and displays the nation's culture, especially its artistic and performance practices. In this case, it is the pre-eminent prestige venue where the culture of the nation can be showcased. It can also serve as a venue for hosting foreign cultures that have been brought to the country. Thus, it can be a place in which intercultural or cross-cultural encounters happen between the nation's cultures and other cultures from around the world. Thirdly, the national theatre can be perceived as an institution for preserving and looking after the cultural heritage of the nation. As such an institution, the national theatre functions as a framework or infrastructural setting for researching, documenting, archiving, propagating, and displaying the nation's cultural wealth.

This chapter is most concerned, however, with the idea of the national theatre as stated in the first and third points above, but before going on to discuss this further, one needs to point out that a great many of the national theatres in Africa—in spite of whatever grandiose and idealist visions, mission statements, and associated political rhetoric with which they began or were inaugurated—almost always, in the end, become reduced to the second category above—that is grand and sometimes prestigious venues for national and international performances and other events. Of the five national theatres looked at here, only the National Theatre in Ghana and the DAC in South Africa, with its associated playhouses and national festivals, appear to be trying to fulfil the three remits of a truly national theatre through their operational structures and activities as stated above.

On the other hand, the National Arts Theatre of Nigeria, when it is functioning, is more of a grand venue than anything else, because there is no evidence of any detailed programme that would help it to function as a cultural institution to achieve the understandings of points 1 and 2. There is not even a mission statement or vision; nor is there a structure that links it to either a cultural policy or other cultural agencies in the country. The main problem with the Nigeria's National Arts Theatre is the lack of continuity that has characterised its activities—most of its past programmes have not been sustained over a substantial period of time for tangible results to be achieved.

The structure of the UNCC in Uganda with the National Theatre attached to it offers a very interesting and potentially effective model, in that it is a national cultural centre with many cultural and arts practices under its mandate, including the National Theatre. However, it is difficult to determine how effective the national theatre is or has been in handling the diverse indigenous performance practices of Uganda. Even the arts village behind the theatre is more of a tourist's market that has only a tenuous link to the National Theatre as an institution for culture and the arts. Where are the schools, training workshops, and facilities to nurture these artists and artisans, so as to improve the quality of their creations?

A national theatre should be much more than a building—it should be a storehouse and an enabling fount for the nation's cultural wealth. In fact, the national theatre should act as a "central bank of culture" that has the task of managing a nation's cultural resources and overseeing the transformation of these resources into cultural capital. Pre-colonial indigenous African societies and cultures have always had the equivalent of a national theatre or a storehouse of arts and culture. A good example is the *mbari* houses of the Owerri Igbo in Imo State of Nigeria.

Mbari, a cultural practice of the Owerri Igbo, in simple terms means "art as sacrifice"—that is art in the service of the community. Every once in a while, when a community is faced with danger, strife, illness, and disease for which it cannot find any cure, the elders meet with the chief priest to divine what the gods want. Usually, the prescription is for an *mbari* house to be built to appease the offended gods. The priest is asked to select talented individuals from the community, who are then mandated to build the house of art for the gods. These men and women are secluded and sequestered from the community for an extended period of time— some *mbari* houses take up to ten years to build. They form a community of artists and crafts people who build the house and fill it with all manner of art works. When they are done, a final celebration is held by the entire community to dedicate the house to the gods as a peace offering to solve the community's problems. Now, the *mbari* idea is of a house where art is made, a house where art is displayed, and a house that represents art in the service of community. According to Herbert M. Cole, "Mbari houses [are] not isolated works of art but [are] monuments growing out of and expressive of, the values and beliefs of Owerri Igbo culture". (1982)

In spite of its deliberate celebration of impermanence, a key philosophy which underpins Igbo arts is that it takes so many years to construct an *mbari* house, and just a year or two for it to fall apart. The main purpose of the building is to honour Ala, the goddess of creation, and thereby ensure the productivity of the earth and the survival of the community. The very short life span of *mbari* houses enables a continued creative engagement with the resources of the earth, while allowing every age group in the village to participate in this eternal cycle of artistic production in the service of life and society.

This could be the basis of re-conceptualising national theatres in Africa. An *mbari* house was more than just a house of art—it was also a house or compound in which art was made and shared. The house encapsulates the Igbo idea of sharing, of collective endeavour, and of a vision about the world and how this world is comprehended and represented. The fact that this house, which sometimes took many years to build, is then left to slowly disintegrate also captures the quintessential Igbo idea of impermanence—life as a continuous cycle of time and things passing, and of generations coming of age and leaving their mark and contributing to the continuity of their community. Each national theatre, in my view, should, in conception and operation, reflect the nation's sense of itself—it should be a place, a context, and a process through which a nation's cultural capital is harnessed and put to the service of the nation and its peoples. Unfortunately, however, this dream will remain deferred until our national policy makers, planners, and national theatre administrators finally embrace a model akin to the *mbari*.

References

Achebe, C. (1983) *The Trouble with Nigeria*. Enugu: Fourth Dimension Publishers.

Babayemi, T. (2011) "Culture is critical to national development." Interviewed by Akintayo Abodunrin [online] Available at: <http://www.cultureindevelopment.nl/News/Discussing_Culture_and_Development/1196/Culture_is_critical_to_national_development> (Accessed 26 May and 2 August 2013).

All Things Ghana. (2012) *PNDC Law 259.* [Facebook] 7 May 2012. Available at: https://www.facebook.com/AllThingsGhana/posts/398706716835622 (Accessed 28 May and 1 August 2013).

Cabral, A. (1974) "National Liberation and Culture." *Transition* 45: pp. 12–17.

Cole, H. M. (1982) *Mbari: Art and Life Among the Owerri Igbo (Traditional Arts of Africa)*. Indianapolis: Indiana University Press.

Collins, S. (2007) "The Growth of a National Form of Theatre in Ghana." [Online]. Available at: <http://www.bordercrossings.org.uk/Articles/SteveCollins.aspx> (Accessed 26 May 2013).

Department of Arts and Culture (DAC). (2006) "Arts, Cultural, Promotional Development." [Online]. Available at: <www.dac.gov.za/functions/ArtsCulturalPromotionalDevelopment.html>. (Accessed 26 May 2013).

Imre, Z. (2008) "Staging the Nation: Changing Concepts of a National Theatre in Europe." *New Theatre Quarterly* 24: pp. 75–94.

Mannoni, O. (1950, 1990) *Prospero and Caliban: The Psychology of Colonization.* Trans. P. Townsend. Ann Arbor: The University of Michigan Press.

Mason, J. D. and Gainor, E. J. (1999) *Performing America: Cultural Nationalism in American Theater.* Ann Arbor: The Michigan University Press.

Memmi, A. (1965, 1974) *The Colonizer and the Colonized.* Trans. H. Greenfeld. London: Earthscan Publications Ltd.

—. (1968) *Dominated Man: Notes Towards a Portrait.* New York: Orion Press.

Okagbue, O. (2007) *African Theatres and Performances.* London and New York: Routledge.

—. (2009) *Culture and Identity in African and Caribbean Theatre.* London: Adonis and Abbey Publishers.

Papp, B. (2012) *The National Theatre in Prague.* [Online]. Available at: <www.panoramio.com/photo/68442603?tag=Prague> (Accessed 26 May 2013).

Schechner, R. and Appel, W. (1990) *By Means of Performance: Intercultural Studies of Theatre and Ritual.* Cambridge: Cambridge University Press.

Shevtsova, M. (1993) *Theatre and Cultural Interaction*, Sydney: Association for Studies in Society and Culture.

South African State Theatre (SAST). (2011) *Annual Report 2010/2011.* [online] Available at: <http://www.statetheatre.co.za/ABOUTUS/HISTORY/> (Accessed 26 May 2013).

Uganda National Cultural Centre (UNCC). (n.d.) "Uganda National Cultural Centre" [online]. Available at: <www.ugandanationalculturalcentre.org> (Accessed 26 May 2013).

CHAPTER FOUR

AFRICAN THEATRE AND THE QUEST FOR AUDIENCE

PATRICK EBEWO AND OFONIME INYANG

Introduction

The issue of the relationship between the audience (as a major stakeholder) and theatre in Africa is something that has been an on-going concern for many years, and is such a worrisome relationship that there is need to interrogate this phenomenon in the public domain. This chapter does not pretend to offer an immediate solution to the sustenance of theatre in Africa, rather it hopes to provoke more serious thoughts about the audience's role in the viability of the theatre enterprise and what people in the performing arts industry and theatre practitioners in particular should do to develop and encourage a continued patronage of African theatre for sustainable development.

The discussions in this chapter are based on the premise that African theatre—unlike its counterparts in Europe and America, or African film and television plays—is a 'poor' theatre in terms of patronage from dedicated African audiences. The task before committed African theatre practitioners of the twenty-first century should be to cultivate and energise a dynamic audience that would promote the theatre industry. The importance attached to the audience as a vital part of the theatre can be seen in the interest generated through research and growing volumes of publications in this sphere of endeavour such as: Bennett, 1997; Lancaster, 1997; Abercrombie and Longhurst, 1998; Olsen, 2002; Brookner and Jermyn, 2003; Reason, 2006; Aaron, 2007; and Balme, 2008.

The relationship between theatre and the audience might often be taken for granted, yet the audience is so pivotal to theatre that without it the theatre as a cultural phenomenon would not exist. In 1977, when one of the authors (Ebewo) was an undergraduate at the University of Ibadan, an introductory course in theatre history that was offered by Professor J. A. Adedeji viewed theatre in the arithmetic terms of "play + players + audience = theatre". Thus, Adedeji emphasised that without the audience, there would be no theatre. It is also in this light that Grotowski defines theatre as "what takes place between spectator and actor" (1968: 32). In the words of Peter Brook, when a person walks across any empty space whilst someone is watching, an act of theatre is engaged (1968: 11 cited in Freshwater, 2009: 1).

In her insightful study, Freshwater avers that the theatrical experiments carried out by directors and many other theatre practitioners during the twentieth century have demonstrated that theatre is not dependent upon its location in a designated building or institution, and that it is possible to do away with plot, character, costumes, set, sound, and script—but "the relationship with the audience provides the theatre event with its rationale" (2009: 2). Concluding, Freshwater argues that this relationship is indispensable for the unique experience that theatre conveys. In essence, "[t]heatre thus provides a connection *both* between the audience and the play *and* between the audience and the performers" (Cameron and Gillespie, 2000: 34).

In theatrical terms, what is an audience? Again, Cameron and Gillespie (2000) aver that audiences are groups of people rather than individuals. They come together at a special place and a special time to watch a performance, and that they affect the way actors perform. In other words, they affect performances. This chapter sees the audience as the major stakeholder and consumer in the theatrical enterprise whose presence is often used to measure the emotional, aesthetic, and economic success of any live performance. The theatre audience is a "social group" that comes together:

> to be entertained, to be stirred emotionally, to be amused by the foibles of their fellow mortals, to be enlightened by fresh insights into the human condition, or to be in the same room with talented interesting people. (Hatlen, 1992: 375)

In this chapter, the audience is not regarded as the occasional, but rather the devoted and regular theatregoers.

Has African theatre built an audience that attends the theatre regularly? This is the question that this chapter sets out to answer. Theatre history has revealed that different eras produce different audiences as social entities in the dramatic experiences. Greek theatre audiences:

were knowledgeable, steeped in their literary heritage, with keen ears for
the rhythm and texture of language, and so thoroughly familiar with the
plays of their time that they could identify specific passages of Euripidean
and Aeschylean dialogue in Aristophanes' comedy *The Frogs*... The
Athenians' search for truth in life resulted in drama that was unflinchingly
and relentlessly honest in confronting evil, suffering and catastrophe.
(Hatlen, 1992: 378–379)

The taste for poetry, pageantry, and action propelled thousands of theatre
enthusiasts to patronise the Elizabethan theatre. The Restoration audience
was made up of "fashionable wits, fops, beaux, parasites, and women of
easy virtue" (Hatlen, 1992: 381). Different places at different times
produce different audiences. What kind of theatre audiences has Africa
produced? What is the nature of the audience that patronise African
theatre?

Live theatre in Africa needs the audience in order to exist, but, sadly,
the audience is gradually declining in some countries, for instance,
Nigeria. Some critics and theatre practitioners believe this decline is due to
audiences' preference for film and television (see Lambert, 2012). We also
suspect that it might be due to the choice of plays, elitism, and expensive
ticket prices. Though there may be lamentations over the declining
attendance statistics at theatres in Europe and America, despite theatre
tickets being booked annually in advance, the African scenario is indeed
more pathetic because it is very far away from making the mark in terms
of audience attendance and theatre ticket sales. Compared with attendance
at festivals and other indigenous performances which are appreciated and
attended by African audiences, conventional theatre in Africa per se has a
hard case to answer. This chapter attempts to chart the way forward for the
survival of an African theatre that is built on the patronage of African
audiences.

Challenges and Impediments

At the Market Theatre in Johannesburg, Zakes Mda, a prolific South
African playwright, mounted a production of *The Hill* (1990)—a play
about migrant labour in Southern Africa, which was supposed to touch the
lives of the exploited black mine workers. A black South African, a friend
of the playwright (Mda), was seen drinking in a nearby pub minutes before
the play opened. Mda demanded to know if he was going to see the play
and the answer was in the affirmative. The play started without the man,
and at the end of the play he was seen enjoying his drinks oblivious of
what had gone on in the nearby theatre. What was wrong? Was the man

harbouring anti-theatre prejudice? The picture painted by this situation points to the fact that there are challenges facing theatre attendance in Africa. What follows is our humble attempt to unpack what we deem to be the challenges which must be overcome in order to keep the theatre afloat as an audience desertification is fast encroaching.

Anti-theatre prejudices should not be deemed to be responsible for the man's resistance to seeing Mda's play. Is theatre and audience attendance thereof alien to African culture? The answer is no. Though theatre-going in the "elitist" European fashion of watching a play in a conventional theatre building may be alien to indigenous African society, the concept of theatre as entertainment and amusement is not in the least alien to Africa considering the fact that indigenous African societies relish their ceremonial outings, festivals, and rituals, with entire communities in attendance. Even in modern-day Swaziland, the *Umhlanga* festival (reed dance) and the *Incwala* ritual celebration are national events that continue to attract participation from Swazi maidens and the entire nation. More importantly, these indigenous performances attract global audiences annually. In late August or early September of every year, the *Umhlanga* sees thousands of unmarried Swazi girls cut and gather reeds to pay homage to the queen-mother and to perform for the king (Joyce, 2009: 5). On its part, the *Incwala* is an annual cleansing ritual when the king acquires supernatural powers for triumphing over evil and all forces of opposition (Ebewo, 2011: 3).

The Concept of Audience in African Theatre

This section interrogates the concept of the audience vis-à-vis African theatre experience. Should African theatre patrons, as a social group, be regarded as audiences in the Western sense of the word? The word "audience" is derived from the Latin verb "audire". Audire implies the act of hearing. Are African spectators at performance sites not more than hearers? Even the Greek audience of the ancient civilisation would frown at this nomenclature because Greek theatre was regarded as the "viewing place"—*theatron*! The term "audience" may not very well suit the African theatre patrons because they are more than hearers—they go to the theatre not only to hear, but to see, ululate, make noise, comment, catcall, boo, whistle, and, if allowed, many South Africans would attend the theatre with their *vuvusela*—a musical instrument (horn) that is used to punctuate the height of the spectators' excitement. Participation by African audiences involves the whole being—they are kinaesthetically engaged.

Therefore, any environment that looks down on the above may deter a "typical African" from attending the theatre.

The Hill was about the miners' plight, but was the familiar *toyi-toyi* (revolutionary chanting) song heard? If the man in the pub had heard the familiar song, which usually culminates in wild dancing, he probably would have dropped his glass of Castle beer and rushed to the scene to see what was going on. But the presentation was a purely academic play, cast in a rather absurd mode with only two actors, an unadorned set, minimal costumes, no make-up, cheerless language, and worst still, no songs or dances were incorporated. And this takes us to the question of what types of plays theatre practitioners are offering contemporary African audiences. Can the choice of plays play a role in attracting audiences to the theatre?

On 14 June 2011, a Nigerian journalist sent an email to krazitivity@yahoogroup.com:

> I am doing a story this weekend on the state of live theatre in Nigeria and would appreciate if you can spare me your thoughts on the live theatre in Nigeria. You would agree with me that the live theatre industry in Nigeria, like the reading culture, has been on the decline for a while. What do you think is responsible for this decline/dearth of live theatre/theatrical performances in Nigeria and probably about the way forward? Do you think the rise of Nollywood has anything to do with the gradual extinction [erosion] of the live theatre culture?

One of the Yahoo! group members responded:

> Thanks for your great effort to revamp the dying live theatre in Nigeria. Left for me, I'd say controversially that the theatre practitioners killed the interest the public used to have in our theatre… I have read several plays churned out by our generation and they are mostly wastework, to borrow from the Chinweizus… Is it the kind of dramas that the Yerimas and the Osofisans write that you think can draw people to the theatre? The long and short of it is that the old theatre practitioners… killed our drama with Marxism bereft of realistic plots, lacklustre themes, etc…. Drama has now become the genre for failed poets and novelists.

Though we do not subscribe to the highhanded tone of the criticism, we feel that we need to sieve the contents of what this respondent is trying to put across. Academic audiences apart, the concern of the writer is that elitist plays with deep-rooted ideological contents may not fare well with the popular audiences. Conventional plays in the Western mode may do well in university theatres in Africa, but may not attract popular audiences. Not many people remember Ola Rotimi for staging *Holding Talks* (1979) or *If: A Tragedy of the Ruled* (1983); instead his popularity rests more on *Our Husband has Gone Mad Again* (1977), *Kurunmi* (1971), and *The Gods are not to Blame* (1971).

Familiar stories that appealed to their popular audiences made Hubert Ogunde, Duro Ladipo, and Kola Ogunmola the cornerstone of Yoruba travelling theatre in Nigeria. Banham writes that "Ogunde not only enjoys the acclaim of popular audiences, but the respect of his fellow—and mostly junior—professionals" (1976: 9). When Ogunde's play, *Yoruba Ronu*—which spoke loudly against Samuel Ladoke Akintola (premier of then Western Nigeria) for usurping power from the popular Yoruba politician, Chief Obafemi Awolowo—was banned in Western Nigeria in 1965, the ban merely illustrated the relevance of the playwright in society, as well as "the huge influence that Ogunde could exert upon audiences through the views and opinions expressed in his plays" (Banham, 1976: 10). It is on record that in the repertoire of Ogunde's plays, it is not only *Yoruba Ronu* that was banned, *Strike and Hunger* (1945) and *Bread and Bullets* (1951) were also banned for "inciting" the public. Ogunmola and Ladipo are reputed to be the fathers of Yoruba Opera, and—like Ogunde—Ogunmola's moral tales "were the staple ingredients of his work and his popularity" (Banham, 1976: 13).

Drama's Impact as a Work of Art

Drama is art, in fact, one of the performing arts. Artists and scholars have struggled for centuries to define art without a consensus. Many have agreed that art is distinguishable from real life by the artist's intention to create or craft something that will evoke a certain kind of response—an aesthetic response—from its audience (Cameron and Gillespie, 2000: 8). Cameron and Gillespie go further to state that though it is difficult to determine the exact nature of an aesthetic response, it "includes an appreciation of beauty and some understanding that goes beyond the merely intellectual or the merely entertaining" (2000: 8). The focus of art is man, and all performing arts have to do with human life in its most intense state (Smiley, 1971: 7). Smiley enunciates some of the identifiable general functions of art to be: generation of new knowledge, production of specific pleasures in human beings, and functioning as a special kind of order in the chaos of life. He goes on to add:

> It offers controlled and permanent beauty. An artist creates by giving diverse materials a controlled form in a skilled manner for a pleasurable end. With each art object, he creates an image possessing unity, harmony, and balance. The artist as creator can give life increased value. (1971: 7)

Without labouring to critique plays and theatre productions, our generation must judge for itself if some of our plays have done justice to the province of arts, and by extension if they have promoted audience participation in theatrical productions.

A Galore of Concepts

In a seeming attempt to become globally relevant, contemporary theatre practitioners in Africa have imported all sorts of labels to garnish African theatre practice. Some practitioners have experimented with avant-garde creations—Ola Rotimi's absurdist play, *Holding Talks* (1979) is an example. The concepts of empathy, alienation as aesthetic distance, sublimation, catharsis, and closure have been latched onto African theatrical practices without adequate interrogation of their relationship with the audience. For instance, it is often the case that the boundary between aesthetic distance and excessive distance is not well defined, in theatrical terms, in most African theatre productions that draw extensively on Western theatre practice. By some of the practitioners insisting on audiences keeping a reasonable distance from the production in order to see the issues raised clearly, they pose a problem for the "typical" African audiences, because many of them are inadvertently distanced from the work of art and are so psychically removed from the work that they have no feelings or thoughts, and as such do not involve/engage themselves with the performance (Smiley, 1971: 253).

Brecht's reaction against empathy as "vicarious emotionality" and his insistence on the state of alienation between the work of art and audience involvement runs parallel to contemporary practice where emphasis is placed on the stimulation of heightened self-awareness. In our opinion, African audiences would prefer to identify with the work, rather than estrangement. The word "alienation" carries a negative connotation as it is commonly associated with "separation" and with what is "foreign". The radical dramatist, Artaud, did not share Brecht's prescription of alienation for the audience. Artaud prescribes what an ideal response from the audience should be:

> It is a question, then, of making the theatre, in the proper sense of the word, a function; something as localized and precise as the circulation of the blood in the arteries or the apparently chaotic development of dream images in the brain, and this is to be accomplished *through involvement, a genuine enslavement of the attention.* (Artaud, cited in Hatlen, 1992: 383; emphasis ours)

Smiley goes on to add that, "[t]he interpretation of catharsis as emotional purgation in *an audience* is as illogical as it is ridiculous. Few, if any, audience member rush to witness live drama because they want a catharsis of their emotions" (1971: 255–256)—and we hasten to add, not many African audiences do as well. Sigmund Freud's experiment with sublimation in the realm of fantasy creation, and the notion of empathy as physiological and psychological responses in the audience are definitely worth exploring in terms of their relationship with African audiences. Empathy is one important constituent of a human being because it is through empathy that the subjective self is related to the objective void—the world we live in (Smiley, 1971: 252). In other words, human beings relate to their environment through empathy—the ability to feel for and share with others.

Contemporary Experimentations

Some African theatre practitioners have dabbled in extreme obscenity and violence in their production of plays. Whether these will promote attendance at productions remains a matter to be investigated. In South Africa, Mpumelelo Paul Grootboom, playwright and director, holds audiences spellbound with extreme violence and nudity on stage. In the fashion of the British *In-Yer-Face* theatre, Grootboom's presentation of sex and violence are indeed apparent in *Foreplay* (2009) and *Relativity: Township Stories* (2006)—plays that are replete with words like "fuck" and "pussy". In his director's notes for *Cards* (2003), Grootboom states that the play has been controversial because of his daring approach, namely the explicit sex, nudity, and strong language. Furthermore, De Vries (2008) states that Grootboom's work often result in some audience members walking out from the theatre because they cannot take the realistic sex and violence.

Arguments have been made regarding whether this sexually explicit and violent type of theatre is obscenity or art, and furthermore whether art can be obscene. Peters (2006: 216) states that the definitional opposition between what is obscenity and what is art, which was developed in the eighteenth and nineteenth centuries, created a classificatory norm, separating the realm of art from the obscene—if a work was obscene, it could not be defined as art, and vice versa.

In the last couple of years, the drama department of one university in Pretoria, South Africa, has repeatedly mounted plays that deal with violence and sex. The *Blue Room* (2011), a play in ten intimate acts by David Hare (a 2011 MA project), handles with reckless abandon the "sexual daisy chain" of ten individuals in search of love and fulfilment of lustful desires. In May 2011, a Master's student in the same department produced *Cleansed*, a play by Sarah Kane. Much more than the mere skeleton of the play was the fact that one female character took all her clothes off in full view of the audience, and a male actor followed suit. The man lay on top of the woman on a bed with "fuck me" moans ensuing from the pair. On a bare floor (beach) was seen a naked male gay couple, engaging in simulated sexual act in full view of the audience. Another tableau shows a topless female strip-tease dancer sitting astride the exposed lap of a male punter and crying, "fuck me" several times. This production caused furore amongst some students and staff members who saw the play, and two staff members volunteered to remove/rework the nudity aspect in the production before it featured at the 2011 National Arts Festival in Grahamstown, Eastern Cape. Even after the play had been reworked, one festival critic wrote:

> Not much needed to be said about the style and approach which tortured the audience with hints of theatre of cruelty, it is blatantly aggressive and hard to ignore. The extremism of the language and images shocks the audience leaving us very unsettled. (Linderboom, 2011)

Though it could be argued that unsettling the audience may be what theatre sometimes aims to achieve, the cultural environment should be taken into consideration.

> ...the audience that is present physically in the theatre is a part of a larger society. This fact has implications for both the practice and the study of theatre. In preparing their art for the audience, theatre artists will inevitably reveal their beliefs about that audience and, incidentally, about the society of which it is a part. It is in this way that theatre (probably more than any other art) both expresses the society of which it is a part and responds to society's pressures, changing its own practices to conform to what society seems to want or need. It is mostly for this reason that theatre is considered one of the humanities and that its study is an important part of a humanistic, liberal education. (Cameron and Gillespie, 2000: 35)

Some may believe that warning the audience beforehand or imposing age restriction would have served the needs of sensitive spectators. Though this precautionary measure might serve a useful purpose, it does not fully address the issue at stake.

Also in 2011, a lecturer in the same institution directed a play titled, *Battlefield*. A battlefield was indeed created with waves of dust and a cacophony of noises that caused discomfort not only to some of the actors/actresses in the play but also some members of the audience, including one of the writers of this essay. A night before the last performance, the head of the academic department received a petition from some cast members stating:

> We, the "Battlefield" cast, are very concerned about our health. The sand we use in the show is giving us allergic reactions. "A" and "M" have already suffered severe asthma attacks after the show, even though they had never been diagnosed asthmatic in their lives. Some of the other cast members are also complaining that it is starting to affect their health and breathing as well... We request that the department arrange for medical precautions—perhaps humidifiers and masks could be provided during performances. (Extract from petition letter by cast members)

On their own merit (as experimental theatre), we have nothing against productions of this nature. But one explanation often given by playwrights and directors of these productions is—"We want to shock the audience!" In a theatre tradition where dedicated audiences need something novel to spice their commitment, this may be tolerable—but in many parts of Africa, where the "modern" theatre may be regarded as a "crawling baby", we must be cautious. In most parts of Africa, where sex in public is regarded as taboo, we need to be very sensitive.

Propriety

Contemporary play production in Africa seems to promote the hegemony of Western theatrical practice. The members of the audience must arrive on time, sit on predetermined paid for chairs, dress appropriately, behave like "civilised" people during the performance—no noise, no chuckles, no cat-calls—and there has to be controlled excitement. In conventional Western theatre, watching a play demands absolute concentration and solemn silence from the audience members. Attention is realised in "spurts" and concentration requires constant renewal because it is impossible for the audience to fix attention on a single object and hold it there as one would a spotlight on stage. Members of the audience usually arrive with the expectation of giving full attention to the play, but if the performance is boring the audience may then escape to another world. Hatlen draws our attention to two kinds of attention—the voluntary and involuntary. The voluntary implies that the audience makes an effort to listen by an act of will, or rather in order to look civilised. On the other hand, involuntary attention requires no conscious effort—it comes as a result of responding to the right stimuli. Good plays should aim at securing involuntary attention from members of the audience (see Hatlen, 1992: 374).

In conventional Western style theatre, reaction in the form of spontaneous applause is discouraged during a performance, and appreciation is reserved for the end—in the form of a standing ovation when the cast take their final bow. In 2011/2012, a tradition emerged from the drama department of Tshwane University of Technology during their performances. When a situation calls for spontaneous reaction in the form of applause, it is immediately checked and suppressed as the "civilised" members of the audience flick their fingers—signalling zero tolerance for noise when a play is in progress. Familiarity with many audiences in Africa shows that people go to the theatre for excitement, mourners attend theatres with the intention of being amused, and any practice that suppresses this emotion is bound to prove inimical to the sustenance of attendance at productions. African audiences do not wait until the play ends to pay wholesale tribute to good performances. Tributes are paid in instalments as the play progresses, and this is why Rotimi once referred to African audiences as "polaroid spectators", a humorous reference to instant cameras—what is known colloquially in some African quarters as "wait-and-take".

Considering the weak economic position of many families in Africa, exorbitant admission fees may hinder attendance at productions. Booking for tickets in advance through the use of credit card facilities and internet resources may also discourage some people from attending a performance. In indigenous African societies, attendance at festivals and public performances was, and still is, free. In the Akwa Ibom State of Nigeria, the Annang and Ibibio communities produce an indigenous theatre known as *eka-ekong* (see Ebewo, 1999). This is essentially a satirical performance that plays a major role in the cultural life of the communities as the song-texts and drama skits aim at ridiculing and denouncing the unwanted behaviour of social misfits, in a bid to improve and amend their lives in their respective communities. This outdoor performance stirs emotions against abnormal behaviour or attitude, thereby arousing mass reaction against non-conformist practices. Members of the audience pay no fees to see the performances because the village head pays for everyone from the village reserve. In contemporary Africa, enlightened local and national governments that appreciate the benefits of theatre should either completely fund audience attendance at performances or subsidise theatre productions and companies. Many national theatres in Europe are highly subsidised (Wilmer, 2008). In the United States of America, many non-profit theatres continue to enjoy generous donations and grants from the

National Endowment for the Arts (NEA) and foundations such as Ford, Rockefeller, and Shubert also sponsor many regional theatres.

Prior to 1994, the South African government established highly subsidised provincial art councils (Performing Arts Company of Transvaal, Natal Performing Arts Company, Cape Performing Arts Board, and Performing Arts Company of the Free State). Though these arts councils were subsidised, they were later regarded as elitist and were re-configured after the collapse of the apartheid government. Currently, the government of the Republic of South Africa has constituted the National Arts Council with the mandate to take the theatre to the people. Apart from state funding of productions to ensure attendance by the generality of the people, grants are made available to theatre groups, particularly those from previously disadvantaged areas with the intention to promote inclusivity and participation.

One of the arguments often put forward in the explanation of why theatre audiences are dwindling in many countries in Africa is that the growth of film and television keeps the audience members at home (see Lambert, 2012). Some critics may argue that the picture painted here is an exaggeration against the background of the resurgence, of some sort, of live theatre in Nigeria and Ghana. In Nigeria, Renegade Theatre is producing sell-out shows at the prestigious Muson Centre in Lagos. In Ghana, James Ebow White and the Royerman Productions are packing out the National Theatre in Accra with their theatre productions. But it must be remembered that these are productions based in urban centres and sophisticated African cities cut off from the reach of the grassroots theatre enthusiasts. Productions that would appeal to many theatregoers should be those that can produce the desired stimulus. In contemporary times, film and television seem to provide the audiences with this requirement—atmosphere and environment—the feeling that an event or a place gives.

> People live for those stimuli which bring about total awareness of life. Such stimuli come from many sources and cause varying reactions. To look at the brilliance of a million stars at night, to feel the surge of sexual love, to watch the face of your child during a happy time – such common experiences may be memorable, live moments. And art too can provide them. At its best, or whenever it achieves its potential for any individual, it causes an intense awareness of life. (Smiley, 1971: 7)

Have we been able to offer our African audiences good dramas that can affect their lives? People attend theatre for various reasons which may be as numerous as the individuals sitting in the theatre. Reasons may vary from theatre taking them to a fantasyland or attendance in order to be in the company of friends. It is the duty of theatre practitioners to give their patrons reasons that are good enough for them to attend the theatre.

Conclusion

We have, to some extent, established that all is not well with African theatre in respect of audience patronage. We have discussed a couple of factors that may militate against audience attendance at performances. To improve upon this situation, theatre practitioners should make sure that the content of the stories in their plays appeal to their audiences—not merely stories or situations that insult or shock them. Theatre must align itself with the cultural demands of the patrons, what the people are used to, and thereafter, meaningful innovations may be introduced. The location of theatres in town centres also discourages popular audiences from attending productions—there are transport fares to consider, the route may not be safe, and the environment may be strange. In indigenous Africa, the theatre goes to the people, rather than the people going to the theatre. The *eka-ekong* theatre of the Annang and Ibibio peoples of south-eastern Nigeria, the *Alarinjo* theatre of the Yoruba people of south-western Nigeria, and the Christmas itinerant players—all travelled to the people. Geoffrey Axworthy exploited this concept when he introduced Theatre-on-Wheels at the University of Ibadan in the 1970s.

In terms of encouraging the audience to attend productions, Theatre for Development (TfD) praxis may play a significant role. TfD practice has been spotted as a potential source of audiences' active participation in African theatre, because it entices them to think about important issues directly impacting their lives (Byram, 1980; Kerr, 1995; Mda, 1993). Its tenets encourage communities to learn new things, acquire facts, and weigh options. It is a participatory medium where information readily achieves social acceptability and the public adopts it without being coerced. TfD is an offshoot of community theatre and operates under the general umbrella of applied drama or theatre.

Many researchers and practitioners of development communication through theatre have advanced positions justifying the role of theatre in development advocacy based on research and experimentation in the field. Zakes Mda (1993) stands out in that group. His position in the field provides a pedestal for orchestrating the failure of conventional media in development communication in Africa. According to Mda, elitist communication systems in Africa serve the needs of a few urban inhabitants, while neglecting those of the vast majority of the population living in the rural areas. The theatre's role in using the people to change their lives, which Mda aptly captures as "people playing people", institutes its capacity as an agent of social transformation. TfD is not the end, but a means to an end in terms of habitual attendance at the theatre. TfD should be treated as an appetiser in the theatre menu, because participation at the level of raising awareness about grassroot problems may attract and expose people to the need to attend productions in the conventional theatre.

Concerted efforts should be made by theatre practitioners to capture the interest of young people in theatre, especially those in schools. The commitments displayed by the Catholic Church benefit from this approach. Right from early childhood, the Catholic Church introduces children to what it calls catechism, a set of questions and answers about the Christian religion. If children in African communities develop a love for theatre, they will grow up into it. The introduction of drama lessons and the promotion of drama performances during Parents' Day celebrations at the primary school level should be encouraged as never before. Schools' drama projects should not only be undertaken because there is available funding to facilitate productions of recommended literature texts, but presentations should be done with a purpose— promotion of interest in drama and cultivation of sustainable audiences for our developing playhouses.

There may be a need to reconsider the unnecessary compartmentalisation of the arts programmes in our schools, particularly at the tertiary level. The practice where dance, music, and drama are stand-alone subjects may not bode well for our theatre industry. In this age, collaboration is necessary and if a stage production incorporates dance elements or music, the result of such a fusion would be more satisfying. These disciplines, after all, are not strange bedfellows because dance and music are among the pillars of what Aristotle described as the "fine arts". Experience has shown that African audiences prefer musicals and dance dramas to theatre productions that depend solely on dialogue. When in 2008 Oliver Mtukudzi, a Zimbabwean musician, collaborated with Ringo Madlingozi, a reputable musician from South Africa, the result was electrifying, and the South African stadium was jam-packed by audience members. When in 1978 the University of Calabar Theatre, Nigeria, collaborated with the Cross River State (Nigeria) Cultural Band, the productions created great momentum, though short lived.

Some stage productions have benefited from the utilisation of multi-media because the latter adds spectacle to a production. Though necessary, the incorporation of film or video strip in a performance must be done with caution as the practice may ultimately push live theatre underground.

If multi-media becomes part of a stage production for the sake of it, an impression might be given that drama cannot exist on its own—that it needs collaboration with modern media in order to survive. If multi-media are incorporated in stage productions without convincing motivation, or merely to "spice up" the stage production, theatre becomes—in the wisdom of Peter Brook—"deadly" (1972: 11–46).

Lastly, theatre practitioners in Africa need to engage seriously in exploratory audience research, in order to scientifically determine what audiences need in view of our subsisting cultures. African theatre needs sustainable audiences, not ad hoc audiences.

> Today we should not look for the few things theatre can be, we are far too gone for that; we should look for the few things theatre must be if it is to live. (Bentley, 1957: ix)

References

Aaron, M. (2007) *Spectatorship: The Power of Looking On*. London: Wallflower.

Abercrombie, N. and Longhurst, B. (1998) *Audience: A Sociological Theory of Performance and Imagination*. London: Sage.

Adedeji, J. (1978) "Alarinjo: The Traditional Yoruba Travelling Theatre." *Theatre in Africa*. Eds. Oyin Ogunba and Abiola Irele. Ibadan: Ibadan University Press. pp. 27–51.

Balme, C. B. (2008) *The Cambridge Introduction to Theatre Studies*. Cambridge: Cambridge University Press.

Banham, M. (with Wake, C.). (1976) *African Theatre Today*. London: Pitman Publishing.

Bennett, S. (1997) *Theatre Audiences: A Theory of Production and Reception*. London: Routledge.

Bentley, E. (1957) *In Search of a Theatre*. New York: Vintage Books.

Brook, P. (1968) *The Empty Space*. London: McGibbon and Kee.

Brookner, W. and Jermyn, D. eds. (2003) *The Audience Studies Reader*. London: Routledge.

Byram, M. (1980) "People's Theatre as Appropriate Media." *Appropriate Technology* 7(2): pp. 21–23.

Cameron, K. M. and Gillespie, P. P. (2000) *The Enjoyment of Theatre*, Fifth Edition. Boston: Allyn and Bacon.

De Vries, F. (2008) "The Man Who Loathes the Label 'Township Tarantino'" [Onine] Available at: <http://freddevries.co.za/archive/2008/09/20/the-man-who-laothes-the-label-township-tarantino.aspx> (Accessed 18 July 2011).

Ebewo, P. (1999) *"Eka-Ekong*: Total Theatre in Annang Folk Art." *Nigerian Heritage: Journal of the National Commission for Museums and Monuments* 8: pp. 85–100.

—. (2011) "Swazi Incwala: The Performative and Radical Poetics in a Ritual Practice." *South African Theatre Journal* 25(2): pp. 89–100.

Freshwater, H. (2009) *Theatre & Audience*. New York: Palgrave Macmillan.

Grotowski, J. (1968) *Towards a Poor Theatre*. London: Methuen.

Grootboom, Paul Mpumelelo. (2009) *Foreplay*. London: Oberon Books Ltd.

Grootboom, N. P. And Chwenwyagae, P. (2006) *Relativity: Township Stories*. Johannesburg: Dung Beetle Dramas.

Hatlen, T. W. (1992) *Orientation to the Theatre*. New Jersey: Prentice-Hall, Inc.

Hay, David. (1998) *The Blue Room*. London: Groove Press.

Joyce, P. (2009) *Cultures of South Africa: A Celebration*. Cape Town: Sunbird Publishers.

Kane, Sarah. (1998) *Cleansed*. London: Methuen.

Kerr, D. (1995) *African Popular Theatre*. London: James Currey Ltd.

Lancaster, K. (1997) "When Spectators Become Performers and Theatre Theory: Contemporary Performances-Entertainments Meet the Needs of an 'Unsettled' Audience." *Journal of Popular Culture* 30(4): pp. 75–88.

Lambert, C. (2012) "The Future of Theatre in a Digital Era: Is the Play Still the Thing?" [Online] Available at: <http://harvardmagazine.com/2012/01/the-future-of-theatre> (Accessed 15 September 2012).

Linderboom, L. (2011) "Cleansed." *Artsmart: Arts News from Kwazulu-Natal*. [Online] Available at: <http://news.artsmart.co.za/2011/07/cleansed.html> (Accessed 4 July 2011).

Mda, Z. (1993) *When People Play People: Development Communication Through Theatre*. London: Zed Books.

Mda, Zakes. (1990) *The Hill* in *The Plays of Zakes Mda*. Johannesburg: Ravan Press.

Olsen, C. (2002) "Theatre Audience Surveys: Towards a Semiotic Approach." *New Theatre Quarterly* 71: pp. 261–275.

Peters, J. S. (2006) Theatricality, Legalism, and the Scenography of Suffering: The Trial of Warren Hastings and Richard Brinsley Sheridan's *Pizarro*. *Law and Literature*, 8 (1): 15-45.

Reason, M. (2006) "Young Audience and Live Theatre, Part 1: Methods,
    Participation and Memory in Audience Research." *Studies in Theatre
    and Performance* 26(2): pp. 129–145.
Rotimi, Ola. (1983) *If: A Tragedy of the Ruled.* Ibadan: Heinemann
    Educational Books.
—. (1979) *Holding Talks.* Ibadan: University Press Ltd.
—. (1977) *Our Husband Has Gone Mad Again.* London: Oxford
    University Press.
—. (1971) *Kurunmi.* London: Oxford University Press.
—. (1971) *The Gods are not to Blame.* London: Oxford University Press.
Smiley, S. (1971) *Playwriting: The Structure of Action.* Englewood Cliff,
    New Jersey: Prentice-Hall.
Wilmer, S. E. (ed.) 2008 *National Theatres in a Changing Europe.* New
    York: Palgrave Macmillan.

CHAPTER FIVE

COLLUSION OR ORGANISED CHAOS?: A SELF-REFLEXIVE JOURNEY TO CHART THE EXPERIENTIAL EXPLORATIONS IN THE SOUTH AFRICAN DEVISING PROCESS

JANINE LEWIS

Introduction

Collaborative composition is essential to theatre, especially to the creative process of devising. Devising[1] is an internationally recognised term assigned to a method of creating theatre that emerged in the 1960s (Oddey, 1994: 8; Heddon and Milling, 2006: 3–6). Devising as a form of creating a production is where the performance originates from collaborative, usually improvisatory, creative enterprise by a group of artists (typically, but not exclusively, the performers). The practice has evolved from the twentieth century to the twenty-first century through the resurgence of the experimental aesthetic traditions of the past to current performance practices (Govan, Nicholson, and Normington, 2007: 4–12).

Devising was originally hierarchal in nature—retaining the ideology of one person's text under another person's direction (Oddey, 1994: 4). This sought to retain the vision of the playwright and favoured descriptive performance or naturalism as the dramatic style. More recently, this has seen a shift. Skilled practitioners in their designated fields come together to develop or create "new work" in collaboration (Oddey, 1994: 8–9; Govan, Nicholson, and Normington, 2007: 4–10). This collaborative theatre-making often incorporates various physical and textual means of articulation, favouring more expressive performance styles as opposed to descriptive ones. Bogart and Landau (2005: 146; Lewis, 2010: 178) define "descriptive" staging as that which fundamentally repeats or re-enacts the external physical and vocal realities, whereas the "expressive" in essence portrays what the experience/situation feels like through abstract physical and vocal realities.

In South Africa, research, oral testimony, yoga and theatre games, exercises, African dance, music workshops, and the study of sociology are some of the strands that have made up the eclectic whole that are incorporated or explored to develop devised plays (Purkey, 1997: 156). It is clear, therefore, that the creative conceptual performance derived from this process does not depend solely on the text or words for its expressive quality, but on the holistic experience that was born from collaborative exploration. Physical interpretive skills are included and vital to this process.

> In performance the workshop [devised] play exhibits a physical quality with a pronounced gestural component which runs alongside and interweaves with the words of the text... (Fleishman, 1997: 175)

In South Africa, collective play-making originated in township theatre and was extensively applied to community theatre practices, as well as to experimental physical theatre. The practice remains collaborative for both applications, but the skills and process of design distinguish them. It would be fair to say that the community practices also favour the more descriptive narrative performance, whereas the physical theatre application lends itself to more expressive forms of performance.

The art of devising is as diverse as the artists and collaborators who are involved in its practice. For most devised performances, the desire is for the collective voice of the collaborating artists to provide a clear concept that articulates the narrative. The stimulation, excitement, and social pleasure of working as an individual within a group initiates collusion, but can very easily turn into chaotic confusion when all participants want to realise their individual focus for the performance as opposed to working towards a common goal. When listening and communication skills are lacking in a group, pandemonium and confusion very often abound.

As a creative approach to the narrative, devising uses improvisation within collaborative explorations. Improvisation lends itself to a sense of structured confusion and chaos. Through improvisation the sense of hurtling the idea of the product towards a theory of chaos forms part of the exploratory practice. Improvised explorations are therefore often non-linear—where seemingly un/related elements combine and are presented through montage and collusion. International theatre companies that utilise the exploratory improvised freedom or "structured un-structure" to create include: SITI Company (New York), Volcano Theatre (Canada), and Frantic Assembly (Wales) amongst many others.

The creative moment of interpretation in improvised performance, generated from chaos, is fleeting. To successfully re-create the dynamic of these "accidental" interactions in performance is challenging to the performer, especially in an ensemble performance. To achieve this re-creation the performer is constantly challenged to "be in the moment" on stage and to re-enact the dynamics of their current situation. Essentially, to re-enact the dynamics of the improvised interaction requires that the performer does not operate in a linear exchange of intention unfolding in time and space, but rather in one that is complex and simultaneously operating. To achieve this requires that a sense of chaos needs to be present. In order to successfully re-create chaos it would then require for it to be organised—which in essence contradicts the purpose of chaos altogether! This chapter will unravel this dichotomy of organised chaos by delving into collaborative expressive performance. The question remains: in order to re-create the dynamic moment in performance, does the shared collaborative authorship between performers/creators require collusion or organised chaos? The chapter will argue that expressive performance requires both collusion *and* a sense of organised chaos.

This essay frames physical actions as expressive performance narratives in contemporary South African theatre. I will argue that collusion and organised chaos are essential elements in the collaborative creative process and are enhanced by expressive performance narratives. Therefore, at the centre of this chapter is the idea of the body in action—gesture, movement, stillness, voice, silence—which does not operate in a linear network but, as indicated earlier, in a complex and simultaneously operating network unfolding in time and space.

In the rest of this chapter, and writing from my unique perspective as both practitioner and scholar, I set out to interrogate experiential explorations in the South African devising process by examining the use of expressive physical action in the Tshwane University of Technology's production of *in our blood* (2011). As part of the unfolding analysis, the chapter will detail the creative, collaborative, and conceptual processes experienced and shared by me as director/creator, with the expressive performers and the participatory involvement of sentient spectators. Also, as a means of charting the collaborative explorations in the South African devising practice the process of re-conceptualising physical storytelling within the production of *in our blood* (2011) will be examined.

Physical or Textual Performance

Contemporary South African performance lends itself to an experiential and participatory methodology in storytelling and collaborative social creativity. At the root of the South African performance experience rests the creative process. For many theatre-makers in South Africa, the written word alone is decidedly insufficient to portray or explain the full complexity of the reality they face. Therefore, at the centre of this essay is the idea of the body in action, as stated earlier.

According to Fleishman (1997: 175), physicality in contemporary South African theatre ranges from formal choreographed sequences to elaborate physical gestures in conjunction with the text. These choreographed sequences may include tribal dances, gumboot dances, *pantsula*[2] dances, or *toyi-toyi*[3] sequences. Consciously conceived physical images created by the director and performers are used to completely replace words when spoken texts are inadequate in conveying the depth of meaning intended in a performance. Fleishman (1997: 182) argues that the theatre in South Africa has often been guilty of simplicity—that instead of clarity, single meanings are presented literally and simply for the audience. He further advocates that rather than the use of literal narratives, alternative methods should be sought where broader options will promote dialogue by demanding an actively imaginative personal response from the spectator. In other words, productions should adopt the application of physicality in South African theatre where the conceptual use of physical actions leads to communication and shared experiences.

Expressive performance allows for the inclusion of inherent physical performance qualities in the process of devising a performance. Already found through performance skills and improvisation, gesture exists before and alongside words as an independent sign system. South African performers are also influenced by an oral tradition that differs from the literary theatre tradition (Ong, 1982: 67). One of the key differences is that oral tradition has a high somatic component as opposed to the conventional literary theatre tradition with its focus on the text:

> The oral word never exists in a simply verbal context as a written word does. Spoken words are always modifications of a total existential situation, which always engages the body. Bodily activity beyond mere vocalisation is neither advantageous nor contrived in oral communication, but is natural and even inevitable. In oral verbalisation, particularly public verbalisation, absolute motionlessness is itself a powerful physical gesture. (Ong, 1982: 67–68)

The communicative nature of physical actions in performance and the meaning transfer from performer to spectator is a key factor to understanding conceptual narratives in a South African context.

> Through a physical oral consciousness meaning may be communicated from the performer to the spectator. The meaning that is communicated can be checked in each spectator's own present experience, influenced by their reference framework and their specific personal-cultural circumstance. (Brook, 1990: 12; also cited in Schechner, 2006: 125)

Examining the creative process through devising explores how physical actions relate to the performer/creator, as well as the spectator.

Devising

Devising offers innovative commentary on, and a representation of, cultural conventions. It strives to find fresh working methods that challenge both the collaborative performer and the sentient spectator through innovative and inventive use of theatre (Govan, Nicholson, and Normington, 2007: 13). The conceptual nature of devising is fluid. It engenders a new experience for every collaborative group of people that come together with the intent of creating a performance (Oddey, 1994: 200; Govan, Nicholson, and Normington, 2007: 4–9; Heddon and Milling, 2006: 3). Oddey (1994: 200) points out that one of the rewards of devising is being involved with a group of people who want to assert their particular views of the world. A key factor in devising is the drawing together of the process of experimentation and sets of creative strategies in order to create a performance (Govan, Nicholson, and Normington, 2007: 9).

One of these creative strategies includes the adoption of a somatic approach in which physicality is explored before textuality. The exploration emphasises creative freedom and openness for both performers and spectators. These experiences in the moment of performance become paramount (Govan, Nicholson, and Normington, 2007: 8), and may also be equated to the improvisations and explorations that take place in the rehearsal space. The inclusion of expressive physicality requires a level of engagement or interpretative participation from the spectator. In contemporary devising performances, the focus on physical actions is akin to what obtains in physical theatre practice. The contemporary physical theatre performer utilises the perception of time and space through expressive compositions in performance. This is because exploring images in time and space through physical experimentation usually unfolds the most honest interactions or transitions found in a production. Physical performance lends itself (both by association and construction) to performance that is as interpretative to a spectator as it is to the performer who is demonstrating the intent in an action. When coupled with layers of text and visuals, it provides depth to the montage.[4]

The intention of this chapter is not to present a comprehensive survey of contemporary practices or a history of montage or devised performances, either globally or in the South African context. Instead, the intention is to look at the modes of artistic practices that are devising, montage, and physical theatre, not as fixed categories but rather as modes of theatre-making that are continually transforming the performance narrative in terms of its experimental, conceptual, expressive, and interactive nature. For the purpose of this essay, my use of expressive staging in the montage process of creating *in our blood* (2011) will be investigated.

in our blood

Who is African? How are we defined? Can we restore dignity and achieve diversity through determining our identity? These are some of the questions asked in the play, *in our blood,* staged at the Breytenbach Theatre by the Department of Drama and Film at Tshwane University of Technology, from 18–26 March 2011. *in our blood* looks to African mythology and folktale to make sense of the current socio-political realities in South African society. It focuses primarily on the stories from the southern African region and acknowledges African gods and goddesses attributed with ancestral knowledge of the creation of Africa (as the beginning of the world) and development of its peoples. Specifically, matriarchal influences are explored to trace the themes of identity, diversity, and dignity.

Source-work and Re/Conceptualisation

The inclusion of the *re-* to the notion of conceptualisation acknowledges the notion that the creative process, or the concept of an artwork or performance, may be in essence a repeat or be occurring afresh/anew. I am working on the premise that there are essentially no new ideas, just new approaches or adaptations in the "current" context.

This interest in reconceptualising creative practices is particularly evident in devising, which has experimented with the limits and potentials of theatre and performance. (Govan, Nicholson, and Normington, 2007: 7)

Source-work is used to provide a *time* and *space* for all the collaborators to fill up with their own reactions and ideas regarding the material or stimuli for the performance (Bogart and Landau, 2005: 164). In the performance process, prior to the rehearsals, the source-work begins when the director/creator identifies a theme or topic and sets in motion the research that would eventually inform the final product. Once collected, the initial formation of the source-work into a scenario is then done conceptually as a continued practice during rehearsals—it constantly informs the process and development of the work.

As a visual and kinetic learner, I find that objects, words or sounds often trigger and create images (moving and static) in my mind— essentially prompting a form of re/conceptualisation. For instance, when I was developing the ideas for the production of *in our blood*, a clear symbol for the issue of lack of tolerance was that of hurtful, hateful words/phrases that are often used to define or characterise anyone considered as the "other" within the South African society. This resulting name-calling and derogatory use of language can be attributed to individuals' need to undermine the "other" in order to raise their own status. I sought to utilise and capture these derogatory terms in an artwork for the performance.

In an attempt to portray how words can contribute to the decay of identity, trust, and diversity I sought to trace fictitious fault-lines across Africa in the form of topographical lines.

In geology a *fault* is a planar fracture or discontinuity in a volume of rock, across which there has been significant displacement... A *fault line* is the surface trace of a fault, the line of intersection between the fault plane and the Earth's surface. (SRK Consulting, 2007: 4)

Drawing these topographical lines reminded me of fingerprint images which link to individual identity. It is worth noting that the lines of a fingerprint are the result of *friction ridges*:

A friction ridge is a raised portion of the epidermis on the fingers and toes (digits), the palm of the hand or the sole of the foot, consisting of one or more connected ridge units of friction ridge skin. (Datasphere Technologies (Pty), 1999)

The terms *friction ridges* and *fault line* led me to define Africa through a fingerprint image (refer to Figure 5.1). The topographical lines were formed using hurtful, hateful words and phrases, and names "spat out" by our many languages in South Africa. The resulting artwork of the *fault-lines* was created on the floorcloth used in various guises in the production, and led to the question: do these words define us?

in our blood

Figure 5-1: The fingerprint drawn as topography lines as utilised in the poster image for the show *in our blood* (2011). Graphic design by Janine Lewis.

Re/Conceptualising Text

The source-work dredged up knowledge surrounding the African gods and goddesses who formed the contextual basis for the characters found in *in our blood*. For instance, the god and goddess characters in the performance includes: *Unkulunkulu*,[5] *Mami-wata*,[6] *Ma-Goddess*,[7] *Medusa the African Queen*,[8] and the *Tree of Life*.[9] Following the source-work, the exploratory physicalisation process then began and ultimately saw the characters come to life on stage.

A variety of artists were invited to collaborate in the creation of this production. Apart from use of multi-media, texts and poetry formed a prominent part of the development of a conceptual scripted scenario from which to begin the rehearsals. Credo Mutwa's (Zulu *sangoma*, writer, and artist) writing was a primary source of inspiration, as was the unpublished works of the *Ancient Stars Trilogy* performances created by Audrey Mullin, Hardus Koekemoer, and Benjamin Botha (2000-2002). Confrontational and repetitive use of poetry was sourced from Makhosazana Xaba and Anni Snyman.

At the heart of the collaborative group were the performers—a cast comprising sixteen senior drama students from the Tshwane University of Technology drama programme. There was a good representation of gender (five women and eleven men) and cultural groupings (Afrikaans, English, Ndebele, Sepedi, Sotho, Swati, Tswana, and Xhosa) in the final cast, achieved through colour-blind casting.[10]

The Expressive Performer/Creator

Through the creative process undertaken by the performers, the conceptual design was able to carry the intended message into the production through the *mise-en-scéne*. The *mise-en-scéne* is an expression to describe the design aspects in theatre. Essentially, it entails telling a story in visually artful ways, including:

> everything that appears before [the spectator] and its arrangement, including composition, sets, props, actors, costumes, and lighting. Blocking of the topography of the performance may also be included. (Thompson and Bordwell, 2003)

For the purpose of composition, descriptive and expressive staging was explored. Suggestions of worlds or environments and imaginative use of basic properties (rather than furnishing the stage with exact replications of real life) allow for a more inventive and stimulating performance. Both the performer and the spectator find it more stimulating to interact with imaginatively suggestive staging. Watching becomes a sensory experience, and the magical and illusionary qualities of the experience become paramount (Lewis, 2010: 187; Callery, 2001: 5).

Initially the *in our blood* cast were not exposed to the conceptual scenario text compiled prior to rehearsals. Instead they were involved with the creative process through explorations and interactive discussions. These explorations also concretised the source-work for all participants, instilling a sense of ownership through collaboration. When it came to the plotting and work with the text, the inherent physical actions and ensemble work were so well established that it was easy to edit and replace much of the spoken words with physical storytelling. An example would be the fight for land acquisition by the various chiefdoms and peoples in Africa. This scenario was achieved through expressive staging that utilised the performers' bodies in time and space—the floorcloth was also manipulated in an effort to assert each chief's dominance, whilst literally going around in circles.

Puppets, Masks and Performing Objects

According to Bell (2001: 5), puppets and masks are central to some of the oldest forms of performance. Proschan uses the term "performing object" to refer to "material images of humans, animals, or spirits that are created, displayed, or manipulated in narrative or dramatic performance" (1983: 4). Tillis further suggests that puppetry should be thought of in three categories:

> tangible puppets, virtual puppets, and stop-action puppets... if the signification of life can be created by people, then the site of that signification is to be considered a puppet. (2001: 178, 182)

Tillis argues, in other words, that the use of animation and audio-visual media—especially in a performative context—may also be considered a puppet.

Moncho's (2011) review of *in our blood* states that the strength of the piece came from the creative techniques applied to the storytelling, these included: puppetry, masks, and performing objects. In line with Tillis' categorisation of puppets discussed earlier, all multi-media (montage and animation) utilised in the context of the production possess possibilities of thought and action, and are as such puppets alongside their tangible counterparts of masks, and performing objects.

Outside the entrance to the theatre, a video montage of war scenes was projected onto the front facade of the building. Chris Taute created this original virtual puppet in response to discussions about themes of intolerance and hatred. The graphic projections were *loud* in their depiction of violence, but intentionally had no sound accompaniment. The virtual puppetry was a silent cry about the atrocities seen, experienced, and inflicted by humans in war. Within the production, a black theatre gauze hung above the audience was revealed when animation was projected onto it near the end of the performance. The animation was *Deep Water*[11], a series of images created by Anni Snyman and animated by Katty Vandenberghe. This *Deep Water* animation was used in the production to portray the character of *Mami-Wata* assuming the guise of a beautiful sexually promiscuous woman.

Tangible or physical puppets also added to the magical performance environment. Tangible puppets took two forms: *Ma-goddess,* a three metre high full-body puppet made from aluminium, plastic, and cloth; as well as *Medusa*, the African Queen (refer to Figure 5-2). In the case of *Medusa,* eight performers worked her gown—raising her up to appear and shift puppet-like in her three-metre by four-metre splendour. The gown mutated from the floorcloth depicting the artwork, *fault-lines,* into *Medusa's* gown, and afterward dissolved back into the floorcloth and was left in a formless heap.

Figure 5-2: (from left) Ma-goddess (Tumi Modise) and Medusa, the African Queen (Lebohang Mazibuko and the cast) from the production *in our blood* (2001). Photograph by Janine Lewis

The cast represented a variety of characters including plants, fish, birds, and various animals, during the scene that depicted the myth of creation. The depiction of the creation scene was done purely with the performers' physicality. When it came to depicting the Big Five[12] wire-art masks were used to assist in the interpretation (refer to Figure 5-3).

> The use of puppetry and animation gave a surreal and nuanced tone to the act. The masks, wired art, and the lighting design only enhanced this. The physical theatre fuelled the plot, but the physicality is layered. At times a number of students would come together and join their bodies in complex positions to portray some kind of animal. The clever use of bodies was fascinating to watch... Throughout the show, you never knew what was coming. The unpredictability of the play kept the audience on their toes. (Moncho, 2011)

in our blood explores African mythology, and so songs and the percussive backing of African drumming were incorporated in some instances as a vehicle for advancing the narrative (Moncho, 2011).

Figure 5-3: (from left) An ostrich, a lion, and an elephant created by the ensemble in the creation scene for *in our blood* (2011). Photographs by Janine Lewis

Once the world, plants, and animals were depicted, the creation scene ended with the formation of humans through the mutation of rolled up "snake-like" forms into human cut-outs worn on the back of performers, as a visual commentary on African fables about how humans evolved from snakes. The civilisation process was then shown through various masks using both conventional and alternative techniques—masks were worn on the top of the head and behind the head, or full-body mask/puppetry. The evolution of humans culminated in the discovery of fire, forming a natural link into an African fable of how *Unkulunkulu* (the great and powerful one) sent fire to humans via the animals. The representation of characters in this advent of fire scene was achieved through performers displaying human characteristics informed by the animals they represented. This was depicted through an appropriate lope in the walk, or dynamics of the animal translated into the body of the human. Figurines made from wire-art adorned with beads were worn on the heads of these characters. The beaded-animals linked the animal and human journey of discovery.

The floorcloth was again used to depict the tethers of chained slaves and held aloft to represent the land from the sea. In the latter instance, the cloth was further manipulated to demonstrate the tribal battles for land by the land-dwellers. Performers on stilts accompanied both instances in which the floorcloth was used. The stilts added to the slaves' shackled appearance and provided eerie clanking sounds to match. The stilts provided height, suggesting hierarchy and power struggles during the scenes where the land and sea-dwellers encounter each other (refer to Figure 5-4).

Figure 5-4: Shaun Koch as a sea-dweller with the boat as a performing object, and the land-dwellers on stilts behind manipulating the floorcloth. From *in our blood* (2011). Photograph by Janine Lewis

The use of stilts and full-body masks and puppets was a contemporary interpretation reminiscent of indigenous African performance practices found especially in the western African regions. All of these effects described above were achieved through a somatic engagement with the devised performance making process. The effects added to the visual communication found in this expressive style of theatre, and encouraged participation from the spectator in the form of interpretation and suspended belief. This interpretation and suspension of belief as a form of participation will be described in the next section titled "engaging the spectator".

Engaging the Spectator

Physical theatre exponent Jacques Lecoq's methodology includes the sense of play and physical character-driven interpretation. In the devising process, this leads to ensemble practice or as Lecoq defines it, *complicité*. *Complicité* has a more complex interpretation than the idea of a shared belief or complicity between performers in an ensemble (Callery, 2001: 71; Murray, 2003: 64). However, what differentiates *complicité* from mere ensemble practice is the inclusion of a shared belief between the performer and spectator that is of crucial importance. The shared belief forges a sense of relationship in which both the performer and spectator "create" the piece together (Callery, 2001: 88, 104; Murray, 2003: 64–65).

The spirit of ensemble only communicates itself to an audience when there is a palpable sense of those performers all being *complicit* (of colluding) in

the deed of daring to create and present a show to the spectators. (Murray,
2003: 71)

In order to achieve this collusive quality between spectator and
performer, the spectator needs to be "cast" in the production as the
audience (Bogart, 2007: 79). The spectators take on a sense of ownership
if they are invited to participate by using their brains and hearts in the
process of experiencing and interpreting a performance (Climenhaga,
2009: 104). "At its core, art is an experience. A work of art asks for
something from the viewer" (Bogart, 2007: 79).

> The spectator needs to be considered as a vital member to the collaborative
> process of creating the production, and their role therefore needs to be
> included from the inception of the process. It is the compelling nature of a
> well-structured and presented composition that draws the spectator even
> deeper into the images presented in a production. (Cummings, 2006: 32)

This essay asserts that the production of *in our blood* is a prime
example of such a well-structured and presented composition devised
through collaboration between performers/creators. The spectators were
encouraged to collude in interpretive creation of the physical storytelling
and expressive staging, and their inclusion into the installation by being
seated on stage was a literal, physical insertion into the performance.
Further evidence of spectator involvement can be traced to the spectators
being encouraged to engage with the production even before the
performance, for instance witnessing the silently seated performers outside
in the parking lot, as well as the video montage projected onto the facade
of the theatre. During the performance, spectators were afforded the
opportunity to interpret the metamorphoses of the performers into the
various characters, which encouraged them to independently select what
and where they wanted to focus their attention, through the deliberate use
of split-focus. Also explored was the close spatial relationship performers
have with the spectators:

> ...in the middle of this, the cast would run towards the audience and
> powerfully recite a poem. This confrontational and repetitive tactic gave an
> edge to the performance, but most importantly it etched these questions on
> one's [the spectator's] mind: Are we responsible for the conflict we see
> amongst ourselves? Do we hold ourselves accountable for it? (Moncho,
> 2011)

Collusion or Organised Chaos?

Devising as a re/conceptual creative practice requires physicality before textuality. The focus on visual communication through expressive staging enhances collusion. Collusion refers to that between the text and the images (inclusive of juxtaposition of the two)—performers as an ensemble and the performers with the spectators by means of the performance. Within the devising process the creators embrace a sense of organised chaos to achieve these collusive relationships. These relationships are achieved when all collaborative participants trust in the process and freely explore within the determined theme. It is this sense of chaos within the process that inevitably yields an honest, exciting product that entices an audience and holds them spellbound.

> The art begins in the crisis of not knowing, and from that not knowing making an action. Picasso said that in a painting you make the first stroke and that the rest of the painting is about correcting that first mistake... in rehearsal you make a stroke and then all the rest of the work is about trying to turn that mistake into something extraordinary. (Bogart, 2001: 34)

The sense of hurtling towards chaos forms part of a larger exploration of a non-linear system, where seemingly unrelated elements combine and are presented through montage and collusion. The creative devising process adopted for *in our blood* saw the performers continuously engaged within the organised chaos. Chaos in the rehearsal process fuelled the endeavour of daring to create and present a show to the spectators. Organised chaos resulted in the final outcome of the production and even continued into each consecutive performance. The organising of the sense of chaos stemmed from the immediacy of being "in the moment" and colluding throughout the performance in order to achieve the visual effect required.

For *in our blood*, these moments of organised chaos could be found in the performance. One such example can be found in the re-creation of *Medusa,* the African Queen's gown, where eight performers crouched, jostled, and sweated within the limited space beneath the floor-cloth, and were literally forced to work together to find their way in the semi-darkness. The eight crouching performers held a ninth performer aloft in this configuration—the only one visible to the audience above the floorcloth (refer to Figure 5-5.). The ninth performer had the added pressure of portraying a haughty character, presented as clearly in control—adapting to the sometimes odd spaces or position she found herself in without letting on about the shuffled chaos going on beneath her gown. This scene was different in each performance. Although basic elements of plotting were maintained, the execution required a sense of organised chaos, where performers are forced to collude in order to achieve their objective.

Figure 5-5: *Medusa,* the African Queen (Lebohang Mazibuko and the cast) from the production *in our blood* (2001). Photographs by Janine Lewis

The spectators only experienced the magical transformation of a flat floorcloth into a three-metre high majestic character that appeared to glide effortlessly around the stage. The energy generated from this organised chaos was channelled towards the character and contributed to a heightened sense of the omniscient dynamic exuded by this puppet of destructive power. The printed words on the *fault-lines* artwork on the floorcloth also appeared to take on a life of their own. The words squirmed and slithered as the cloth moved. These hateful words contributed to *Medusa*'s destructive power dynamics and were reminiscent of the snake-like dreadlock protrusions from her head for which she is infamous.

As a social message, the idea of collusion and chaos may be further extended to the theme of *in our blood*. Humanity colludes continuously. The negativity generated from pessimistic collusion can be destructive and result in chaos, where people are being riled and rallied in frenzied crowds that only produce conflict and devastation in their wake.

Conclusion

Physical theatre lends itself to a sense of *complicité*, both in the process of making and in the rendition of the product/ion. There is a sense of collaborative or shared authorship by all those involved in the theatre-making process. The spectators are also often invited into the creative process through interpretive meaning-making. *Complicité,* therefore, offers an influence on the devising model by way of physical theatre within a South African context.

For the purpose of re/conceptualising physical storytelling, a sense of ensemble was palpable among the performers for *in our blood*. Without it, the performances could not have transpired. The ensemble was developed through the exploration processes (including improvisation) undertaken in the rehearsal phase and further enhanced by the sense of ownership and pride that each cast member felt for the performance. The inclusion of the spectator as a collaborator strengthened the shared belief between the performer and spectator, and helped to achieve the collusive quality of *complicité*. This is because the complex dynamics of collusion ensures that the meaning-making is shared through communication between creative performer and sentient spectator, necessitating *complicité*. In other words, at the root of the contemporary South African devised theatre experience rests the practice of *complicité*.

Through explanation of the creative processes involved with *in our blood*, this chapter serves to confirm that the experiential explorations generated from the devising process necessitate both collusion and organised chaos. Both collusion and chaos offer a personal liberating experience of freeing the imagination through devising and montage creative processes in collaboration, which may also be socially advantageous. Such social advantages may arise from the collaborators' interpretation of inherent metaphors and analogies through the lens of their personal and cultural standpoints as a way of encouraging dialogue between all participants. This means that to achieve both collusion and chaos within a performance, *complicité* is required. To re-enact the dynamics of ensemble interaction in performance, it is required that the performer/creator achieves a complex, simultaneously operating network in space and time, through collusion. Also, in order to successfully re-create this collusion with the spectator, a sense of organised chaos is required.

Africans have been utilising collusion and organised chaos as intrinsic elements in their theatre-making for generations, by telling stories where singing, dancing, live music, and audience participation are essential. The excitement can be thrilling, which makes this kind of theatre a truly liberating experience for both the performer and spectator. South African performance lends itself to this quality of experiential and participatory performance in storytelling and collaborative social creativity. In other words, contemporary South African performance is intrinsically experiential and participatory, and makes the most of its magical meaning transfer through physical expressive staging and *complicité*.

Notes

1. Also termed devised theatre, devised performance, collaborative creation (USA), or workshopping (RSA).
2. *Pantsula* is a dance originating from the South African townships. It focuses primarily on the legs and feet and is invariably performed in soft shoes, *tekkies* (sneakers). The Zulu word *pantsula* means to "waddle like a duck" or alternatively "to walk with protruded buttocks", which is a characteristic of the dance (Harper, 2011).
3. *Toyi-toyi* refers to the militant dance and chanting found in the protest marches in South Africa. It is a colloquial term that encompasses all energetic dancing and crowd hype associated with mass demonstrations, and is still relevant today. Rumoured to have had its origins in Zimbabwe, *Toyi-toyi* dance includes high steps performed by protesters and is accompanied by the singing and chanting of slogans (Blackstone, 2008).
4. The montage concept was originally coined by Russian filmmaker, Eisenstein, to indicate how any two pieces of films stuck together inevitably combine to create a new concept. But in juxtaposition, a "new" dramatic effect is created by cutting and rearranging snippets of sensation and experience. These contrasting shots or sequences are used to effect emotional or intellectual responses.
5. *Unkulunkulu* refers to the Zulu description of the ancient and powerful one. He is the all-knowing one and is likened to *Cagn,* the creator god of the Bushman, also known to the Khoi San as *Utixo*. He is the great and powerful one! (Lynch and Roberts, 2004: 130; Leeming, 2010: 296–297; Lang, 2007: 146). He does not have the same name as the Zulu name given to God as we know today. *Unkulunkulu* was never revealed in a human form in the production *in our blood.* Instead, his omnipresent voice was all that "embodied" him.
6. *Mami-wata* are ancient African deities whose primordial origins and name can be traced linguistically through the languages of Africa formulated in ancient Egypt and Mesopotamia. *Mami* is derived from "ma" or "mama", meaning "truth/wisdom". *Wata* is a corruption of the ancient Egyptian word *Uati* meaning ocean water and the Khoi San *Ouata* meaning water. In ancient Egypt, Isis was worshiped as *Mami Uati*—the "self-creator", "the one who reigned alone in the beginning" and known as the "unmarried (or virgin) mother". After thousands of years, *Mami wata* has survived in west African *Vodoun* and other African religious systems. The original phonetic form has changed very little. *Mami wata* has inspired many followers throughout the African diaspora (Zogbè, 2007a, 2007b; Drewal and Houlberg, 2008). *in our blood* depicts *Mami wata* as the water goddesses of healing and fertility, who often assumes the guise of a beautiful and sexually promiscuous woman— depicted through the *Deep Water* virtual puppet.
7. *Ma-goddess* or *mother goddess* is a term used to refer to a goddess who represents motherhood, fertility, and creation. Egyptian *Met* or *Ma'at* (Monaghan, 2010: 32). She embodies the bounty of the earth. When equated with the earth or the natural world, such goddesses are sometimes referred to

as *mother earth* or as the *earth mother*. Many different goddesses have represented motherhood in one way or another. Some have been associated with the birth of humanity as a whole. Others have represented the fertility of the earth (Mutwa, 1998; Monaghan, 2010: 32). *in our blood* depicts *ma-goddess* as a totem Venus fertility doll—similar to the symbols found as far back as the Palaeolithic Age. Ma-goddess was a three-metre high full-body puppet made from aluminium, plastic, and cloth. She is voluptuous and sports a *steatopygia* (fat bottom) common among some African cultural groupings, especially among southern African Khoi and San (Bushman and Hottentot) women. *Ma-goddess* is seen wearing a loincloth, the traditional attire of the early Khoi and San people.

8. *Medusa* means "sovereign female wisdom". Medusa—*Metis* in Greek—was actually imported into Greece from Libya where she was worshipped by the Libyan Amazons as serpent-goddess. *Medusa* was the destroyer aspect of the great triple goddess also known as *Neith* (Egyptian), *Anath* (Semitic), *Athene* or *Ath-eena* in North Africa, and *Athana* circa 1400 BC Minoan Crete (Ryan, 2006: 67; Root, 2007: 62, 91). In images of *Medusa*, her hair resembles dreadlocks showing her origins in Africa. Legends told that that if you were to look upon her face you would glimpse your own death, because *Medusa* saw your future (Root, 2007: 62). *Medusa* has historically been seen as the archetype of the nasty mother; however, she is far more complex. She symbolises the cycles of time as past, present, and future: the cycles of nature as life, death, and rebirth. She is universal creativity and destruction in eternal transformation, guardian of the thresholds between the realms of heaven, earth, and the underworld. She destroys in order to re-create balance. She purifies. As crone she consumes by devouring all on the earth plane. Through death we must return to the source, the abyss of transformation, the timeless realm. We must yield to her and her terms of mortality (Ryan, 2006: 67; Root, 2007: 62).

9. Tree of Life is traditionally known through the symbol of a *Baobab* tree in Africa. The *Baobab* is also known as the "upside down tree". These trees are known to live for thousands of years in the drier savannahs of Africa and are associated with many legends. The "tree of life", connecting all forms of creation, is often associated with the "tree of knowledge" that is said to connect heaven (with the branches of the tree) and the underworld (through the roots of the tree). Both are forms of the world tree or cosmic tree. According to some scholars, the "tree of life" and the "tree of knowledge", of good and evil portrayed in various religions and philosophies, are the same tree (Mutwa, 1998; Watson, 2007: 154). *in our blood* traces the tree of life fable as told by Credo Mutwa in his book *Indaba, my children* (1998) where the "tree of life" and the mother goddess had a turbulent relationship, yet are credited with creating the humans and populating the earth. Depictions of the tree in *in our blood* as uprooted, mangled, and bandaged, echoes a statement made by Rose Francis about South Africa:

In a nation with so many sores dressed in Elastoplast, the festering grows... treatment is not denial but a draining of the pus. Gangrene is an insidious disease!

10. The Tshwane University of Technology drama programme has an open casting policy for all their annual student productions. This results in a simulated workplace practice exercise akin to where everyone has an equal chance at an audition in the industry. The most appropriate actors are therefore selected on their ability and suitability to the production and may see a conglomeration of students from various levels pitted together in one cast. The process is further enriched when students in practice learn from working in conjunction with other performers with a variety of skills.
11. Refer to:
http://www.annisnyman.co.za/2010/content/artGallery/watDeepWater.htm
12. The Big Five refers to five of southern Africa's wild animals: lion, leopard, elephant, buffalo, and rhino. They originally earned their special reputation by their great size, as well as the danger they represented as trophy animals.

References

Bell, J. (2001) "Puppets, Masks and Performing Objects at the End of the Century." *Puppets, Masks and Performing Objects* (2nd Edition ed.). Ed. J. Bell. New York: New York University and Massachusetts Institute of Technology.

Blackstone. (2008) "Power to the People: The Toyi-toyi of South Africa." *African Business Daily*. (18 February) [online] Available at: <http://power-2-people.blogspot.com/2008/02/toyi-toyi-of-southern-africa.html> (Accessed on 20 July 2011).

Bogart, A. (2001) "Anne Bogart." *American Theatre* 18(6): p. 34.

—. (2007) *And Then, You Act: Making Theatre in an Unpredictable World.* New York and London: Roultledge.

Bogart, A. and Landau, T. (2005) *The Viewpoints Book: A Practical Guide to Viewpoints and Composition.* New York: Theatre Communications Group.

Brook, P. (1990) *The Empty Space* (2nd ed.). Harmondsworth: Penguin.

Callery, D. (2001) *Through the Body.* New York and London: Routledge.

Climenhaga, R. (2009) *Pina Bausch: Routledge Performance Practitioners.* London and New York: Routledge.

Cummings, S. (2006) *Remaking American Theatre: Charles Mee, Anne Bogart and the SITI company.* Cambridge: Cambridge University Press.

Datasphere Technologies (Pty) (1999). "Fingerprints." [Online] Available at: <http://woiSA.com> (Accessed 21 September 2010).

Drewal, H. and Houlberg, M. (2008) *Mami Wata: Arts for Water Spirits in Africa and its Diasporas.* Los Angeles: Fowler Museum at UCLA.

Fleishman, M. (1997) "Physical Images in the South African Theatre." *Theatre and Change in South Africa.* Eds. G. Davis, and A. Fuchs. New York and London: Routledge.

Govan, E., Nicholson, H., and Normington, K. (2007) *Making a Performance: Devising Histories and Contemporary Practices.* London and New York: Routledge.

Harper, C. (2011) *The History of Pansula Dance.* [Online] Available at: <http://www.ehow.com/about_5414725_history-pantsula-dance.html> (Accessed 20 January 2011).

Heddon, D. and Milling, J. (2006) *Devising Performance.* Hampshire and New York: Palgrave Macmillan.

Lang, A. (2007) *The Making of Religion.* (UK, Ed.): Echo-library.

Leeming, D. (2010) *Creation Myths of the World: An Encyclopedia* (2nd ed.) Vol. 1. CA: ABC-CLO, LLC.

Lewis, J. (2010) "Physical Actions as Expressive Performance Narratives: A Self-Reflexive Journey." Eds. M. Munro and M-H. Coetzee. *South African Theatre Journal (SATJ) Special Issue: Movement and Physical Theatre in South Africa* 24: pp. 175–200.

Lynch, P. and Roberts, J. (2004) *African Mythology A to Z* (2nd ed.). New York: Chelsea House.

Monaghan, P. (2010) *Encyclopedia of Goddesses and Heroiness.* CT: Greenwood Press.

Moncho, K. (2011) "It's Unpredictable, it Will Keep You on Your Toes." *Tonight: What's on.* (24 March) [online] Available at <http://www.iol.co.za/tonight/what-s-on/gauteng/it-s-unpredictable-it-will-keep-you-on-your-toes-1.1046315#.UfnU95AaKUk> (Accessed 26 March 2011).

Murray, S. (2003) *Jacques Lecoq, Routledge Performance Practitioners.* London: Routledge.

Mutwa, C. (1998) *Indaba, My Children.* Edinburgh: Payback Press.

Oddey, A. (1994) *Devising Theatre: A Practical and Theoretical Handbook.* London and New York: Routledge.

Ong, W. (1982) *Orality and Ilteracy: The Technolgizing of the Word.* London: Metheun.

Proschan, F. (1983) "The Semiotic Study of Puppets, Masks and Performing Objects." *Semiotica* 47(1/4): pp. 3–46.

Purkey, M. (1997) "Tooth and Nail: Rethinking Form for South African Theatre. *Theatre and Change in South Africa.* Eds. G. Davis and A. Fuchs. New York and London: Routledge.

Root, I. (2007) *Redeeming the Gorgon: Reclaiming the Medusa Function of Psyche.* MI: ProQuest LLC.

Ryan, A. (2006) *The Goddess Guide to Chakra Vitatlity* (2nd ed.). [online] <http://www.goddess.com.au> (Accessed 15 August 2010).

Schechner, R. (2006) *Performance Studies.* New York and London: Routledge.

SRK Consulting. (2007) "Specialist Study: Geology and Seismics." *ESKOM Holdings Ltd Generations Devision—Specialist Study for Scoping Report.* Limpopo. 28 September 2007, pp. 1–41.

Thompson, D. and Bordwell, K. (2003) *Film Art: An Introduction.* (7th ed.). New York: McGraw-Hill.

Tillis, S. (2001) "The Art of Puppetry in the Age of Media Production." *Puppets, Masks and Performing Objects* (2nd ed.). Ed. J. Bell. New York: New York University and Massachusettes Institute of Technology.

Watson, R. (2007) *The African Baobab.* South Africa: Struik.

Zogbè, M. (2007a) *Mami Wata: Africa's Ancient God/dess Unveiled* (3rd Edition ed., Vol. 2). Martinez, GA : Hunter-Hindrew, M.V.

—. (2007b) *The Sibyls: The First Prophetess' of Mami (Wata).* Martinez, GA: Hunter-Hindrew, M.V.

CHAPTER SIX

BLACK FEMALE DIRECTORS IN SOUTH AFRICAN THEATRE

KARABELO LEKALAKE

Introduction

During the apartheid era in South Africa, white theatre practitioners got the opportunity to produce, direct, and perform plays that were subsidised by the government (Van Heerden, 2008: 26). Circumstances forced the black theatre practitioners to pursue the ideals of prominent cultural activities, such as the Black Consciousness Movement and protest theatre, to express their anger. As a result of the racial segregation, protest plays were performed in community halls, church halls of the blacks, or during opposition rallies, primarily because the regime that governed the country in that period did not agree with the contents of the protest plays (Loots, 1997: 143). Black male South Africans were at the forefront of creating plays that demonstrated their unequivocal objection to the apartheid regime (Orkin, 1991: 230).

Plays such as *Sizwe Banzi is Dead* (1976), *Woza Albert!* (1983), *We Shall Sing for the Fatherland* (1993), and *Egoli* (1980), dealt with matters that affected the oppressed black people, and—as indicated above—these plays were written, directed, and performed by men. Playwrights of black theatre marginalised black female theatre practitioners by predominantly creating male characters. At the time, the social perception of a black woman was nothing more than as a mother, sister, daughter, wife, or a widow. Black women also became accustomed to playing second fiddle to their male counterparts: they were homemakers and caregivers. Their capability in the creation of protest theatrical productions was overlooked; hence the platform of storytelling was predominantly used to put men in the limelight

There was a small fraction of black women, however, that were as
nationalist in character as black men. Socio-political factors, such as the
oppressive government and claim to supremacy by their male
counterparts, provoked these women to fight for social justice. There were
also black female theatre practitioners who were active in rejecting the
system that oppressed the black people in general. Their efforts as
playwrights and directors of protest plays, presented the majority of black
women with a platform to express their grievances. Now, this chapter will
take a cursory look at the outstanding theatre works created by black
female forerunners in South African theatres before 1994.

Black Female Trailblazers in South African Theatre before Democracy

Theatrical works by black female dramatists such as Gcina Mhlope's *Have
You Seen Zandile?* (2002), Fatima Dike's *So What's New?* (Mda, 1996)
and Magi Williams *Kwa-Landlady* (Perkins, 1999) told stories of the
unheard voices of black women. These playwrights primarily created
plays that endeavoured to address social issues, specifically those affecting
women. During the time of apartheid, the notion of a black woman
directing a play was something unimaginable, therefore it rarely took
place. It is known that these women, and many other women that aspired
to create plays, were faced with several difficulties—they were censored
by the apartheid government, and their duties as nurturers, wives, mothers,
and daughters kept them away from the theatre.

The year 1986 marked a milestone in the history of black women in
South Africa theatre. *You Strike a Woman, You Strike a Rock* (Kani, 1994)
was the first protest play created by black women against the apartheid
regime that wanted to enforce the extension of pass laws[1] on black
women. The emancipation of women and gender equality were the main
themes of the play. This play articulates the struggles of black women
during apartheid and encourages women to rise against the idea that they
are second-rate to men. Orkin explains that this was the one play that
represented women and staked their existence in the theatre (1991: 230).
However, it is interesting to note that even though the content of the play
focuses on the plight of black women, on its premiere, it was directed by a
white woman, Phyllis Klotz.

With the democratisation of South Africa in 1994, like many things,
the theatre industry experienced radical changes. According to Temple
Hauptfleisch, these changes influenced key areas such as: the themes of
plays, venues, professional status of performers, and the nature and

preference of the audience (1997: 160). Black theatre practitioners began with lamentations for a transformed theatre industry. Even though the country's post-apartheid constitution brought a sense of assurance, there was a need for immediate and tangible change.

In August 1996, a government White Paper on Arts, Culture, and Heritage was published by the Department of Arts and Culture (DAC), which aimed to redress the imbalances of race and gender in the theatre industry. The Performing Arts Council (Performing Arts Council of the Transvaal, Cape Performing Arts Board, Natal Performing Arts Council, and Performing Arts Centre of the Free State), that specifically benefited white people, had to be transformed into playhouses. According to Van Heerden (2008: 26), the purpose of these Performing Arts Councils was to "nurture and advance white elitist, typically with a Eurocentric culture and aesthetic focus". The change was relevant since it was to afford black theatre practitioners an artistic platform to celebrate their cultural heritage, while benefiting from the new dispensation.

At present, it is approximately eighteen years since the initial publication of the White Paper on Arts, Culture, and Heritage that advocated equal rights for all practitioners irrespective of race or gender. However, there seems to be a predicament of a dearth of black female directors in South African theatre. The questions that arise are: has the document served its purpose? Has it presented black female directors with equal opportunities, just as to those of white people in general and black men? In this chapter, I argue that both white and black men, together with white female directors, continue to dominate the mainstream theatre to the exclusion of black female directors.

Contemporary Black Female Directors in South African Theatre

In search of black female directors in South African theatre—who currently direct plays on the mainstream platform—I came across three directors that seem to be prominent in their own right. They are singled out as having made their mark in directing theatre productions through hard work. I conducted interviews with them to get their perspective on the state of South African mainstream theatre regarding black female directors. In this segment, I will narrate the impressive contributions of these black female directors.

Ntshieng Mokgoro is an outstanding contemporary black female director in South Africa today. Mokgoro acquired her training at the Market Theatre Laboratory in Johannesburg. In 1998, she became a

Market Theatre Laboratory fieldworker that scouted for talent in the Gauteng area. Mokgoro is one of a few black theatre practitioners who came up through the ranks—rising from being a librarian that frequently read books to children, to becoming a theatre director. With her artistic talent, she claimed her position as one of the few professional black female theatre directors in South Africa. Mokgoro said she got into directing because she was angry at the South African theatre world for side-lining women and ignoring their concerns. In a newspaper article, she notes:

> until quite recently, women would play supporting or minor roles, leading to frustration until they quit the production, feeling used and cheated. (cited in Dlamini, 2008: 3)

This constitutes a rather bold statement by Mokgoro that might articulate the views of many black female practitioners who think only privileged males access the mainstream theatre.

With the kind of stories Mokgoro tells, one gets the sense that she embraced the role of a director simply because she wanted to assert herself as a woman who tells stories about being a black woman in South Africa. Her fascination with writing about the myths of women, birth, arranged marriages, and the death of women could reflect the trials that several black women have experienced in South Africa. *Thursday's Child* (2008) is the epitome of the kind of stories that intrigue and are eventually penned by the dramatist. The play is based on the life of a young girl who is forced into destitution and a life of abuse and squalor. She becomes a prostitute when her mother abandons her.

With a very simple and yet intricate set and costume, Mokgoro used her directorial expertise to present an eloquent piece composed of powerful images on stage. She tells a literal tale using ordinary things like oranges, carrots, milk, and blood that create aesthetics on stage. With her experimental directorial signature, Mokgoro creates unique pieces of work. While interviewing Mokgoro, she commented on her directorial approach in *Thursday's Child*:

> I wanted to fuse three different directing styles of theatre; abstract, physical and symbolism. Rape has been done a number of times on our theatre stages; I wanted to present it in a different way. (2010)

After directing *Thursday's Child* in 2008, Mokgoro had the distinction of being the first black female director to win a prestigious award of the Standard Bank Young Artist in the drama category. This naturally brought affirmation to the dramatist's career, that indeed she was doing something right. She explains the accomplishment as "a wonderful recognition to be noted as a professional director, receiving the award felt like a stamp of approval" (Mokgoro, 2010). It is worth noting that even though Mokgoro has written and directed a number of theatrical productions, such as *Umdlwembe* and *Veil of Tears* (both unpublished), it took this award for her to be recognised as a professional director. That said, it is discouraging to Mokgoro that attaining the Standard Bank Young Artist Award is not recognised by everyone in the industry. Seemingly, she still battles to get her plays in to state-funded theatres. Speaking at the Women in the Arts Speak Workshop, hosted during the *Zwakala Community Theatre Festival* at the Market Theatre, on 18 December 2010, Mokgoro contends:

> I am tired of being an emerging director. I have been emerging for the past 10 years. When I won the Standard Bank Young Artist of the Year Award, part of that was that I got to present a play in the mainstream but the industry still treats me as an emerging director. How do you eventually stop being an emerging artist?

According to Mokgoro, transformation is slowly taking place in the industry. Black women are seen getting executive positions as theatre producers and administrators, but the position of a theatre director in the mainstream is still really hard to break into. Preliminary research on plays produced by the state-funded theatres in South Africa indicates that Mokgoro's statement is accurate. There are more plays directed by white theatre makers than those by their black counterparts. During a previous interview I conducted with Mokgoro on 11 March 2009, she stated that:

> there is still a division when it comes to race and gender. There is great support shown towards white directors because they are always directing shows.

Warona Seane is another black female director of note. She is a formally trained dramatist that has the ability to mount prolific theatre productions with great eloquence. In 1995, she received her performing certificate at Cape Academy of Dramatic Arts, an institution affiliated with the Trinity College of London. Taking a cursory look at Seane's artistic works—such as *Fragments of an Orgy* (2006), *Mute Echoes* (2007) and *For the Coloured Girls Who Have Considered Suicide When the Rainbow is Not Enuf* (2008)—it is evident that this black woman has reached great heights in South African theatre. Her directorial style, which requires actors to depend on their bodies and not the set to tell the story, afforded her the opportunity to stand out amongst many directors in the industry. Her directing approach commits to a distinct signature which reveals her vast experience in the field of theatre.

In 2010, Seane directed the play *Eclipsed*, written by Danai Gurira, at Windybrow Theatre in Johannesburg. The script depicts the story of the Liberian Civil War that arose in defiance of Charles Taylor's rule and its negative impact on the female population of the region. The story is told through dark humour, it presents women who are oppressors. For someone who has been practising in the theatre industry for more than a decade, *Eclipsed* was the first play directed by Seane to be produced by the state-funded institution for the mainstream platform. In an interview in 2010, Seane stated:

> I started directing after completing my degree in 1999. Ten years later, I get the opportunity to do a professional piece, where actors are paid professional fees and the production is done on a good budget.

While others might contest the idea that the industry does not discriminate between men and women, there are obvious signs of the existence of such an imbalance in relation to black female directors:

> Yes, there are imbalances, in more ways than one, but women contribute to these imbalances. I mean just the other day I invited theatre practitioners to attend one of the *Eclipsed* rehearsals where we could later engage in a critical dialogue about the show. Theatre practitioners that came through were men only. There were no females that attended the session. If we as women do not stand together as a united force, then we will not be victorious. (Seane, 2010)

To a certain degree, Seane may have a point. It is imperative for black female theatre-makers to support one another and it is expected of the black female forerunners—such as Gcina Mhlope, Fatima Dike, Maggie Williams, and Thoko Ntshinga—to support contemporary directors as they understand the dynamics of the industry better. But if there are no platforms for such interactions, the process of mentoring young directors cannot take place. Seane goes on to explain the circumstance of black female directors in South African theatres as unfortunate:

> I think black female directors are at an unfortunate era where there is no Barney Simon. We miss someone like Barney Simon, someone who is constantly searching for new talent, someone who is looking to develop a practising artist to a greatest female theatre maker. It is unfortunate

because we do not have anyone like that. A lot of white female directors'
rose during the Barney Simon era. (Seane, 2010)

This is an interesting observation by Seane, particularly when one
considers the critical role played by Barney Simon in the development of
South African theatre. Simon was a playwright, director and philanthropist
that was passionate about working with multicultural artists to create
plays. Perhaps most black female practitioners are staying away from
theatre because people like Simon or developmental programmes that
nurture young talents are now scarce. At the 2010 Women in the Arts
Speak Workshop, Seane acknowledged that funding is an issue that
confronts both men and women in the theatre. However, she argues that
the sector has little faith and little support for female-led productions.

Napo Masheane is the third and final black female director to be
discussed in this chapter. Masheane made her mark in South African
contemporary theatre as a renowned poet, playwright, producer, actress,
and director. Over the years, she has exhibited an impressive talent for
theatre. Like many other female theatre artists, Masheane had feared, at
some points, that her efforts to get her shows into mainstream theatre was
an impossible dream to realise. Even though Masheane has her foot in the
industry, she believes that there are still not enough black female directors
in South African theatre.

Masheane has a directing style, which she defines as "broad" because
she fuses the language of poets and the acting ability of her actors;—
however, she is best known as a producer. This might have been what
caused a delay to her eminence in her career as a director. In 2009, she
wrote and directed *Fat Black Women Sing* which was performed at the
Market Theatre. The play gave the audience a fly-on-the-wall insight into
women's views about food, sexuality, love, experiential hurting, loss of
self-worth, and motherhood issues. *Fat Black Women Sing* is told through
dialogue and the astounding vocal abilities of five full-figured women. As
the women share their stories and their secrets, they peel away the layers
of "ugliness" associated with being ugly, which is defined by their outer
appearance as fat individuals. With this production, Masheane encourages
women to value themselves regardless of how they look or are perceived
by others.

Talking about Masheane's directorial journey in mainstream theatre,
there is a sense of resilience from the director. She is of the opinion that as
a black female director you always have to work twice as hard as male
directors. According to Masheane, as a black female director, you are only
as good as your last project, last play, or last script (2009). When I asked

her if there were enough black directors compared to white directors, she said:

> If they were there I would not be pushing myself to do the work I do. If they were there I would not feel alone and lost. If they were there I could be part of that community and have millions of points of references. I have to do what I do because there are not many of us. Our industry is dominated by the white community of directors and black men. I can count ten black men who are known directors and writers. Show me at least five black women who have produced, written and directed top plays in this country in the last five years? (Masheane, 2009)

Masheane is of the strong view that prominent black male theatre practitioners are not helping in the development of their female counterparts in the theatre industry. When I enquired about the role of black male directors in South Africa, she said:

> They are not known to ensure that black females start to assume roles of play directors, has one of the male practitioners actually mentored a young female director?

She is convinced that mainstream theatre tilts gender and race scales heavily in favour of black men and white people. Her articulate concern about the condition of black female theatre practitioners is another example that theatre in South Africa is imbalanced.

Evidently, there are a significant number of white female directors who create outstanding works, but it is difficult for black female directors to produce plays on the mainstream stages. Based on the analysis of these three black female directors in South Africa, it is obvious that there is some form of discrimination towards black female directors. However, it is still difficult to ascertain the factors that contribute to the dearth of black female directors in mainstream theatre. Looking at their various experiences in the process of establishing themselves as play directors, there is evidence of a number of issues that undermine black women's role as theatre directors in South Africa.

Finding Black Female Directors in South African Theatre

In 2008, I had a thought-provoking discussion with a male theatre practitioner, Tebogo Maboa, on the apparent scarcity of black female theatre directors in South Africa. He was of the questionable opinion that there are no black female theatre practitioners who could successfully direct plays (Maboa, 2008). Even though Maboa went on to acknowledge the directorial work of Ntsieng Mokgoro—which he describes as "an attempt"—he equally argues that is as far as his knowledge of black female directors goes. At that time, it was interesting to see that Maboa used the word *attempt* to describe Mokgoro's work. Continuing, he claims, "I personally feel that women are afraid of the challenge. They do not want to come forth and expose their works in theatre." Maboa's sentiments might be a reflection of how black female theatre practitioners are wrongly assessed by other theatre practitioners within the industry. His statement is careless and fails to take into consideration the challenges that most black female directors might encounter.

In another interview with Malcolm Purkey (2008) who was then the artistic director of the renowned Market Theatre, we discussed the position of black female directors in contemporary South African theatre. I asked him why there were hardly any plays directed by black women on mainstream platforms, such as the National Arts Festival and state-funded institutions. In response, a question was directed to me instead. A question to which, I gave a spontaneous reply. Purkey challenged me to mention at least five prominent black male directors in South African theatre. "James Ngcobo, Mncedisi Shabangu, and Paul Grootboom," I answered. Instead of mentioning five established black male directors, I could only mention three. The more I thought of what to say, the more it became difficult to readily come up with more names. This provocative discussion alarmed me and brought me to the realisation that there is indeed a greater concern.

I then evaluated the 2008 National Arts Festival (NAF) programme for mainstream theatre. It became apparent that out of the nine plays that were showcased that year, only three of those plays were by black male directors: Martin Koboekae directed *Biko*, Mncedisi Shabangu directed *Ten Bush*, and Itumeleng Motsikoe directed *Waiting*. It was rather disappointing to see that there was not even one theatre production by a black female director. However, in 2009, Ntshieng Mokgoro emerged as the only black female director and James Ngcobo as the only black male director in the mainstream programme during the NAF. Mokgoro directed *The Olive Tree*, a play based on the story of four generations of women, each one carrying the sins of their mothers forward into their own lives. Again in 2010, there was no play directed by a black woman, but Aubrey Sekhabi and Mandla Mbothwes were the only black directors in the mainstream programme with their productions of *Rivonia Trial* and *Inxeba Lomphilisi* respectively. Perhaps, Masheane's earlier utterances on how black male directors are failing to support emerging black female directors should be disregarded. It seems as though black male directors have struggles of their own too.

In researching the dearth of black female directors, it became evident that there is a great variety of mainstream theatre productions directed by a handful of white female directors. The list includes Lara Foot-Newton, Janice Honeyman, Tina Johnson, Sylvaine Strike, Claire Stopford, Yael Farber, Janni Younge, and Lara Bye. These directors have undoubtedly established their names and their works in the South African theatre industry. On the one hand, their shows are produced in state-funded theatre venues around South Africa. As a result, there is a great manifestation of white female productions in the mainstream domain. On the other hand, there seems to be an insignificant number of black female directors creating works in state-funded institutions. In the following segment, I will analyse possible factors that appear to keep black women away from directing on the mainstream stage.

Shifting the Paradigm of South African Theatre

The perennial debate on transformation regarding gender and race equality within the theatre industry indicates that there are discrepancies in the White Paper on Arts, Culture and Heritage. Evidently, the role of black theatre practitioners has undergone significant change in South African theatre since 1994. Transforming structures to allow black arts practitioners to manage the four state-funded institutions demonstrates a momentous change in the theatre industry. The Windybrow Theatre is now under the management of Vuyo Maphela; Linda Bukhosi is the chief executive officer at the Durban Playhouse; Annabelle Lebethe was appointed as the chief executive officer of the Market Theatre in 2011; and Xoliswa Nduneni-Ngema headed the South African State Theatre from 2008 to 2012. As black women themselves, the position that Bukhosi and Lebethe occupy indicates a positive development in the role of black women in the industry. However, these changes might be considered as trivial if they are not cascaded to other levels of the industry which remains unbalanced in terms of gender and race.

It appears as if the South African theatre industry is still far from achieving true equality since the end of the apartheid era. Based on the interviews I have had with the black female directors, it is evident that they are not presented with the same opportunities as their black male or white counterparts. Going forward, this chapter will explore three major factors that contribute to the dearth of black female directors in the mainstream theatre. I investigated these three factors in the hope of understanding the evident scarcity of black female directors in South African theatre today.

Support from State-funded Theatre Institutions

State-funded theatre institutions in South Africa appear to be following the trend of using the same directors. The work of directors such as Malcolm Purkey, Lara Foot-Newton, Marthinus Basson, Mark Fleishman, James Ngcobo, Janice Honeyman, Paul Grootboom, William Kentridge, Lara Bye, and Aubrey Sekhabi seem to be prominent in these theatres. In this instance one cannot help but ask two questions: do prominent directors guarantee a full house during performances of plays? Or are the theatre institutions deliberately marginalising black female directors?

In her defence of the Market Theatre, Tshiamo Mokgadi—who is the institution's producer—said at the Women in the Arts Speak Workshop in 2010, "there is an inferiority complex on the part of some black women in the arts" (Harimbi, 2011). This statement presents a contentious view of black female directors, since there is no proof to back-up Mokgadi's outrageous claim. She also contends that the Market Theatre is faced with financial and resource challenges, arguing that: "We would love to produce everyone's shows—if we had enough staff, money, space and other things". Mokgadi goes further to explain that funding is less, therefore it is hard for them to put on twenty-three to twenty-five shows a year. During that workshop, Mokgoro repudiated what Mokgadi said by stating her co-producing experience with the Market Theatre:

> I feel black female directors are victimized in your institution. When you approach Malcolm Purkey, all you get is "we will see if someone cancels a show" or "you can bring your piece but you have to get rid of so-and-so".

Mokgoro asked Mokgadi how she could get rid of an actor when she was working with her from the beginning. Explaining further she notes that the Market Theatre dictated whom she could work with and that she was not willing to compromise on her preferred actors. Seemingly, on the 29th of October 2011, I interviewed Malcolm Purkey to get his view on the lack of black directors in South African theatres. Purkey responded to the above incident during the interview. He was of the view that Mokgoro wanted to do the play with a specific actor who was not good enough for a specific role. He said:

I explained to Mokgoro that some things with the production did not work, but she was not willing to re-evaluate the decisions she had made as a director.

This squabble is a reminder that one of the objectives of theatre institutions is to be commercially viable. At the end of the day, the producers have the final decision as to which plays they want to produce so that they can make money. However, the prerogative of the director is to decide whom they want to feature in a production they are directing. When producers impose conditions regarding whom the director can cast in a play, the director may lose perspective with regard to the way in which she has envisioned the play. Perhaps in this instance, Purkey did not demonstrate confidence in Mokgoro as a director. This observation made me to think of Masheane's argument that:

> The truth is white people want us to do what they what us to do. When theatres are asked to consider us, they feel it might be risky or that they need to establish the saleability of the production (Khuthala, 2008: 33)

I referred back to the White Paper on Arts, Culture and Heritage (DAC, 1996) to see what the task of state-funded institutions should be. The document states that institutions have a responsibility to:

- promote the full range of art forms, cultural activities and heritage;
- develop cultural industries;
- wider access to arts, culture and heritage promotion and development.

Unfortunately, this is not the case when it comes to some state-funded theatre institutions. In a discussion on the role of theatre institutions in promoting black female directors, I interviewed Claire Stopford who is a well-established white female director and actor, and she observes the following:

> I do not think enough initiative was taken to develop keen and rising black female directors. If we look at the Market Theatre and the history of this institution, then I can say that the company is not doing enough to create space to develop black artists. The institution's objective has shifted from a place that searched for talent to a place of producing plays that can only make them money. The Market Theatre is headed by two white men, Malcolm Purkey and Graig Higginson. I feel they are not creating opportunities for black people that are talented and need guidance and mentorship into the process of developing. (2010)

It is obvious that the structure of the state-funded institutions have difficulties implementing some of the policies contained in the White Paper. It is also apparent that the Department of Arts and Culture (DAC) is not doing enough to ensure transformation in the industry. Maurice Podbrey, former artistic director of Centaur in Montreal, Canada and now a South Africa based theatre director puts forward the notion that the government is failing theatre practitioners irrespective of their gender and race. He argues that the South African government is failing to use money budgeted for development programmes to nurture artists that have potentials (Podbrey, 2008). This observation seems to be popular among many theatre practitioners in South Africa, and in considering Podbrey's comments in view of the position of black women directors in South African theatre, it is evident that the DAC has failed this group of theatre practitioners particularly. It is not necessarily the government, but the state-funded theatre institutions, that are failing the artists. For example, the Performing Arts Centre of the Free State is one institution that has dismally failed theatre practitioners. Over the years, it has failed to develop one black female director. The institution has the financial resources to develop theatre makers but it has not invested its resources to produce one notable black female director in the province.

Women Need to Tell Their Stories

The same trend that was evident during apartheid, of women not writing their stories, seems to be going on even after democratisation. In her anthology of *Black South African Women* (1999), Kathy Perkins puts forward a view that tries to articulate the position of black women in South Africa by collecting their stories. She observes that while the stories by, and about, women are often told by their male counterparts, there is a tremendous absence of literature written by women about their own lives (1999: 2). I discovered that this was indeed true. Consequently, for a very long time in South African theatre, men had the advantage of telling women's stories. The depiction of women in plays like *And the Girls in their Sunday Dresses* (1993), *The Game* (2008) and *Sheila's Day* might not adequately represent the lives of ordinary women because they are told from the men's point of view (Perkins 1999:145). This is unfortunate because black women did not have the platform to tell their stories. It is then questionable whether the male playwrights did justice to the characters in these plays. Perhaps the playwrights' decision on the portrayal of female characters is irrelevant at this point—the real issue is who interprets those female stories on stage.

In Solberg's *Alternative Theatre in South Africa*, Maishe Maponya eloquently articulates the need to have black women telling their stories when he argues that:

> Those who have the sensitivity and the expertise to address the issue of gender in their work must be given the space to do that. We cannot continue to impose our male conceptions on women's issues. (1999: 187)

You Strike a Woman, You Strike a Rock is an example of a text that supports Solberg's hypothesis. The play was conceived by a trio of black female practitioners—Nomvula Qosha, Thobeka Maqutyana and Poppy Tsira. However, a white woman, Phyllis Klotz, directed the stage production. Over the years Klotz has directed this play in mainstream theatre venues. The play demonstrates issues that affect women in the black community. Evaluating the period of conception of this play, it is justifiable to say apartheid circumstances dictated the terms of who could direct the play. At the time, it was safe to have a white woman leading a group of black women who wanted to articulate their experience of being oppressed by the apartheid system. However, one would question whether the directorial interpretation of a white woman, from a different socio-cultural background, truly reflected the world of oppressed black women during apartheid. Also, why is it that since this play was written, it has never been directed by a black female director for a mainstream theatre? Perhaps established black female directors have delayed their progress in the industry by simply staying away from telling their stories.

In order to change the dynamics of South African theatre, black women have to take ownership of their stories. Currently, there is a dearth of black female playwrights—therefore it becomes a seemingly unattainable process to try to get black female directors on to the mainstream stage. There should a vanguard of black female playwrights to guarantee that the voice of black women is heard in the theatre. Moreover, to guard against the emanation of stereotypical or incomplete stories of black women, the black women themselves have to take responsibility for writing their stories and directing them. Both Masheane and Mokgoro create opportunities for themselves to direct plays by writing their stories, and perhaps this is a route that every emerging black female director should take at this stage in the development of South African theatre.

The Necessity to Acquire Formal Qualifications

Acquiring proven practical experience and formal qualifications in directing is another element that helps with the progression of one's directing career in South African theatre. Mokgoro and Masheane share the sentiment that if an emerging black female director does not have the relevant academic training, despite being capable, their work will not get the acknowledgment it deserves. Masheane said:

> The commercial circuit is hard to fit into. You need authorisation and validation from theatres and of course, academic qualification (Khuthala, 2008: 33)

This might be true if one considers that most white female directors that are prominent in South African theatres have an academic qualification or some form of formal training. Also, comparing the measured success of an emerging black female director, Princess Zinzi Mhlongo, who has a qualification in theatre, to the professional progress of Mokgoro and Masheane, it might be true that formal training is essential. Mhlongo directed Zakes Mda's play, *And the Girls in their Sunday Dresses,* at the State Theatre in 2008 and at the Market Theatre in 2010. In 2011, she presented Fatima Dike's *So What's New?* at the Market Theatre. Princess Mhlongo has continued to rise in prominence within South Africa and, in 2012, she won the Standard bank Young Artist Award for drama. She presented *Trapped* which she wrote and directed for the National Arts Festival. As the director of *Trapped,* Mhlongo was selected as one of four young international directors at the 2012 Salzburg Young Directors Project in Austria.

Talking to Mhlongo about her position as an emerging black female director, she clearly expresses her passion to succeed in what appears to be a male dominated industry. During an interview, Mhlongo said, "I knock on doors and I know eventually someone will open the door" (2010). Her break-through came from the South African State Theatre when she was offered an opportunity to direct Mda's popular play; *And the Girls in their Sunday Dresses.* During the interview, Mhlongo explained that it is important to her to create plays: "I understand that not everyone will like my work but I direct shows regardless". She acknowledges that having a formal qualification in theatre gives her anadvantage over someone who has not trained formally.

The observation by the black female theatre practitioner Gcina Mhlope, however, rightly puts the point of formal training into question. In Khuthala's newspaper article, Mhlope notes that she was sucked into the field of directing because unfortunately drama students get little support from theatre institutions to bring their theories to life (2008: 33). If this is the case, why do some theatre producers make formal training a prerequisite to directing on mainstream platforms? Both Masheane and

Mokgoro explained how they lost out on directing opportunities because they did not have a formal qualification. Yet, someone like Seane, with a formal training background, still encounters difficulties when it comes to directing plays on the mainstream stage.

My personal experience as a qualified, emerging black female director can also tell a different story. Trying to get into the mainstream theatre from the Performing Arts Centre in the Free State (PACOFS) has been daunting, and yet encouraging. The reputation of the PACOFS is not a good one. The state-funded theatre institution is notorious for embezzling state funds. After countless proposals to stage productions at this institution, I can confirm that having a formal qualification is not necessarily something the institution takes into consideration in making these decisions.

Conclusion

This chapter does not, in any way, endeavour to start a battle of the sexes in theatre, or to distinguish between plays that black and white people do. The objective of the chapter has been to mirror the occurrences in South African theatre pertaining to the transformation for black female directors in the mainstream scene. The chapter also aims to show that the White Paper on Arts, Culture, and Heritage (DAC, 1996) does not yet serve its purpose. Previously, black women experienced double oppression from their male counterparts and the apartheid regime. Like their black male counterparts, they encountered hindrances in producing their plays in state-owned playhouses. The agents of the then apartheid government censored their protest plays and constantly hounded them, but they remained undaunted and persevered in finding avenues for staging their plays. There has been a constant and on-going marginalisation of black female practitioners in South African theatre. If they had not been convinced about what they had set out to do, they would have easily given up.

As was pointed out earlier on, the three highlighted black female directors succeeded through sheer hard work. They also remained fearless and resolute in their efforts to tell their stories on the mainstream theatre stage. It seems that contemporary black female directors inherited the issues and difficulties that their predecessors encountered. With no holds barred, and from where I am standing, I asked these directors whether the resources and opportunities in South African theatres are accessible to everybody. Yes, resources and opportunities are available but there remains the big question of how they are distributed. Without doubt, black women are, more than ever before, better placed to write about themselves and the society at large. They need to take the first step; women have to take charge of their own advancement. Keketso Semoko, a theatre practitioner and television personality, gets to the heart of the matter when she observes:

> It's not about women versus men. It's got to do with the credibility that you bring with you and not competing with men. Go out and do what you do and do it right. Let's not wait for someone else to do it for us. (Herimbi, 2011)

It is encouraging seeing an emerging theatre director like Princess Mhlongo, practising her craft on the South African and international platforms and doing exceptionally well. There are also other promising and qualified directors such as Keamogetswe Moeketsane from Pretoria and Jessica Lejowa in Johannesburg, who are still managing to showcase their works without any budget or the need to use professional actors. Moeketsane noted in an interview with me that she still finds the industry challenging:

> When you are young and a woman, people do not take you seriously until they have seen your work. If you are a male director things just happen easily. (2011)

With the evidence from the study discussed in this chapter, it would seem that the White Paper on Arts, Culture, and Heritage is misleading in its intentions towards black female theatre practitioners. It appears as if the state-funded institutions still apply the policies that governed the previous Performing Arts Councils. At this point, it seems the only logical step is for the South African government to implement a strategic policy that will ensure there are developmental programmes for black female directors to emerge and flourish. The South African theatre industry has to adopt the workable policies to facilitate the development of emerging and aspiring directors in general. Once these developmental initiatives are available, the black female directors have to advance their craft. Nevertheless, theatre practitioners and the government need to stop living under the pretentious umbrella that South African theatre is balanced, otherwise we will never experience full transformation in the sector.

Notes

1. Pass laws: an apartheid regulation enforced by the regime to segregate black people from white people. This law required black people to produce their passbook at all times. This book indicated the identity of a person, where they worked, and where they resided. A black person that did not have a passbook during apartheid would be arrested and detained. The passbook limited the movement of black people.

References

Department of Arts and Culture (DAC). (1996) *White Paper on Arts, Culture and Heritage.* [Online] Available at: <http://www.dac.gov.za/white_paper.htm#CHAP1> (Accessed 16 March 2010).

Dike, F. (2011) *So, What's New?* Performed at Market Theatre. Johannesburg. Directed by Princess Mhlongo (28 June 2011).

Dlamin, N. (2008) "Coming Out From That Hell of All Hells." *City Press* (24 February): p.3.

Fugard, A. Kani, J. Ntshona, W. (1976) *Sizwe Bansi is Dead* and *The Island.* New York: Viking Press.

Grootboom, P. and Dube, M. (2010) *Rivonia Trial.* Performed at Graema College, Grahamstown. Directed by Aubrey Sekhabi (20 June 2010).

Gurira, D. (2010) *Eclipsed.* Performed at Windybrow Theatre, Johannesburg. Directed by Warona Seane (5 August 2010).

Hauptfleisch, T. (1997) *Theatre & Society: Reflections in the Fractured Mirror.* Pretoria: J.L. van Schaik.

Hauptfleisch, T. and Steadman, I. (1983) *South African Theatre: Four Plays and an Introduction.* Pretoria: HAUM Educational Publishers.

Herimbi, H. (2011) "Sisters Need to Do It for Themselves, Theatre Discussion is Told." *New Age* [online] 11 January. Available at: <http://www.thenewage.co.za/mobi/Detail.aspx?NewsID=7688&CatID=12> (Accessed 20 February 2011).

Higginson, C. and Shabangu, M. (2008) *Ten Bush.* Performed at Rhodes Box Theatre Grahamstown. Directed by Mncedisi Shabangu (3 July 2008).

Kani, J. (1994) *More Market Plays.* Johannesburg: Jonathan Ball Publishers.

Khuthala, N. (2008) "Female Actors Still Looking On From the Curtain of the Stage." *City Press* (24 February): p. 33.

Koboekae, M. (2008) *Biko.* Performed at Victoria Theatre, Grahamstown. Directed by Martin Koboekae (3 July 2008).

Loots L. (1997) "Re-Remembering Protest Theatre in South Africa." *Critical Arts: A South-North Journal of Cultural & Media Studies,* 11(1 &2): p 143.

Maboa, T. (2008) *Women in Theatre.* Interviewed by Karabelo Lekalake. Informal interview at Windybrow Theatre in Johannesburg, 20 March 2008.

Manaka, M. (1980) *Egoli: City of Gold.* Johannesburg: Ravan Press.

Masheane, N. (2009) *Being Black, a Woman and a Director.* Interview by Karabelo Lekalake [email] 20 April 2009.

—. (2009) *Fat Black Women Sing.* Performed at Market Theatre, Johannesburg. Directed by Napo Masheane (18 February 2009).

Mbothwe, M. (2010) *Inxeba Lomphilisi.* Performed at Graeme College, Grahamstown. Directed by Mandla Mbothwe (24 June 2010).

Mda, Z. (1993) *And the Girls in their Sunday Dresses.* Johannesburg: Witswatersrand University Press.

—. (1996) *Four Plays.* Cape Town: Vivla Publishers.

—. (2001) *We Shall Sing for the Fatherland and Other Plays.* Johannesburg: Ravan Press.

Mhlongo, P. (2010) *Directing in South Africa.* Interviewed by Karabelo Lekalake. Group discussion at National Arts Festival in Grahamstown, 3 July 2010.

—. (2012) *Trapped.* Performed at Rhodes Theatre, Grahamstown. Directed by Princess Mhlongo (28 June 2012).

Mhlope, G. (2002) *Have You Seen Zandile?* Pietermaritzburg: University of Natal Press.

Moeketsane, K. (2011) *Emerging Black Female Directors.* Interviewed by Karabelo Lekalake. Structured recorded interview at the South African State Theatre in Pretoria, 26 March 2011.

Mokgoro, N. (2008) *Thursdays' Child.* Performed at Market Theatre, Johannesburg. Directed by Ntshieng Mokgoro (27 February 2008).

—. (2009) *Black Female Director in South Africa.* Interview by Karabelo Lekalake via-email, 11 March 2009.

—. (2009) *The Olive Tree.* Performed at Graeme College, Grahamstown. Directed by Ntshieng Mokgoro (6 July 2009).

—. (2010) *Creating Plays.* Interview by Karabelo Lekalake. Structured interview at Windybrow Theatre in Johannesburg, 29 August 2010.

Mtwa, P., Ngema, M., and Simon, B. (1983) *Woza Albert!* London: Methuen Ltd.

Ndlovu, D. (2008). *The Game.* Performed at Drama Playhouse Theatre, Durban. Directed by Duma Ndlovu (29 July 2008).

Orkin, M. (1991) *Drama and the South African State.* Manchester: Manchester University Press.

Perkins, K. (1999) *Black South African Women.* Cape Town: University of Cape Town.

Podbrey, M. (2008) *The Lack of Black Female Directors in South African Theatres.* Interviewed by Karabelo Lekalake. Structured interview at the National Arts Festival in Grahamstown, 3 July 2008.

Purkey, M. (2008) *The Position of Black Women in South African Theatres.* Interviewed by Karabelo Lekalake. Structured interview at the National Arts Festival in Grahamstown, 3 July 2008.

—. (2011). *The Lack of Black Female Directors in South African Theatres.* Interviewed by Karabelo Lekalake. Structured recorded interview in Johannesburg, 29 October 2011.

Seane, W. (2010) *Your Journey as a Director and Working on Eclipsed.* Interview by Karabelo Lekalake. Structured interview at the Windybrow Theatre in Johannesburg, 14 August 2010.

Solberg, R. (1999) *Alternative Theatre in South Africa.* Pietermaritzburg: University of Natal Press.

Stopford, C. (2010) *The State of South African Theatre Pertaining Black Female Directors.* Interview by Karabelo Lekalake. Structured interview at the National Arts Festival in Grahamstown, 23 June 2010.

Van Heerden, J. (2008) "Theatre in a Democracy: Some Major Trends in South African Theatre from 1994–2003." PhD Thesis: University of Stellenbosch.

Wentworth, M. (2008) *Waiting.* Performed at Victoria Theatre, Grahamstown. Directed by Itumeleng Motshikoe (26 June 2008).

CHAPTER SEVEN

PORTRAYAL OF WOMEN IN THE WRITINGS OF NEW GENERATION NIGER DELTA DRAMATISTS

CHRISTINE ODI

Introduction

The handling of gender issues in Nigerian literary works was for a long time the exclusive preserve of male writers whose portrayals of female characters is informed by their patriarchal view. The Nigerian patriarchal society, like most African societies, is a social system that arrogates social power to men in every important institution, while women have no real access to power. Women in patriarchal societies are, therefore, constrained by socio-cultural norms that attempt to keep them perpetually subordinate to their male counterparts.

The re-emergence of feminist and women's liberation movements in the 1960s led to renewed agitation for the rights of women in the Western world. The movement then spread to other parts of the developing world as more scholars embraced feminist ideologies to support women's empowerment struggles in their various societies. Consequently, in the African dramatic scene, female writers began to espouse feminist viewpoints and challenge established notions of female subordination in African societies.

Most of the early dramatic works emanating from the Niger Delta, in consonance with the larger patriarchal Nigerian society, were written by male dramatists who advanced accepted patriarchal ideologies of their society. The Niger Delta region has, in the recent past, come under national and international scrutiny owing to youth restiveness and protests against multinational oil companies and the Federal Government of Nigeria for their gross exploitation, negligence, and underdevelopment of the oil producing areas. The degradation and destruction of the region's land and water resources, arising from the negative effects of the oil companies' exploration activities, have led to the loss of the people's means of subsistence. This is in addition to the federal government's neglect of the development needs of the region. These issues weigh heavily on women in the region who still have to contend with cultural practices that continue to deny them their fundamental human, political, and social rights. Furthermore, the Niger Delta woman's existence is threatened by the militant activities of the youths, as well as the regular invasion of their communities by the military.

Every dramatic writing, according to Lanre Bamidele, "emanates from within the context of an environment and the playwright being a social historian chronicles events that shape his/her society" (2000: 34). The new generation of writers whose works reflect these socio-political realities have not given sufficient focus to the rights and privileges of the Niger Delta woman, neither are the roles of female characters in the context of feminist rights in the twenty-first century properly portrayed in the dramatic works of these emergent playwrights. These issues will constitute the thrust of this chapter.

The Niger Delta Region of Nigeria

The Niger Delta region is a typical coastal wetland located in the southern part of Nigeria. The area lies in the Equatorial rain forest whose climatic conditions consist of the rainy and dry seasons. The vast volumes of water and extremely dense vegetation predetermine the peoples' major economic activities, which are fishing and farming. Other economic activities of the people include: canoe carving, distilling of alcoholic spirits sourced from palm wine, and lumbering.

Politically, the region comprises six states, namely: Akwa Ibom, Bayelsa, Cross River, Delta, Edo, and Rivers states. These six coastal states are all oil producing states. The Niger Delta region is one of the least developed in the country, in spite of the massive oil wealth the country derives from the area. Ironically, the exploration and exploitation activities of the multinational oil companies in the region have caused immense devastation to the Niger Delta environment. This condition deprives the people of their traditional economic occupations. The oil companies' indifference to the adverse impact of their activities on the environment and on the people, and the federal government's perceived complicity, have consequently led to militancy and youth restiveness in the region.

The activities of the militant groups led to the federal government's initiation of the amnesty and post-amnesty programmes, intended to empower youths in the various communities that make up the Niger Delta. While the offer of amnesty resulted in the denunciation of violence by most of the erstwhile militants, the post-amnesty programmes that followed are yet to address the underlying issues of degradation of the environment and underdevelopment of the region. The people still cannot go back to their traditional economic activities, which have been negatively impacted upon by the devastation caused by oil and gas exploration (Ibaba, 2005; Binebai, 2010).

The Niger Delta Woman

Every individual is a product of a society and the society is in turn shaped by its culture. The Niger Delta woman, being a product of culture, is born into a society that has cultural structures designed to keep her silent and passive. Culture not only excludes her from political decision-making processes in her society, but also denies her access to certain fundamental rights. She is subject to cultural practices that undermine her dignity as a human being, some of which are: widowhood practices, female genital mutilation, preference for sons, lack of equal educational opportunities, early marriage, and teenage pregnancy. She is merely considered as an appendage of male members of her society, in the sense that she is recognised as a person only in relation to whose daughter, wife, or mother she is.

The Niger Delta woman, shaped by her environment, is an industrious, hospitable, and pragmatic woman who engages in fishing and farming activities to cater for the needs of her family. Her primary and sole cultural purpose is to ensure the wellbeing of her family, a role she has been playing effortlessly for generations. The negative impact of oil exploration activities on her environment, the ancillary human atrocities caused by youth agitation, cultural practices, and—for a long time—denial of access to education, have all contributed to deprive the Niger Delta woman of her rights, and the opportunity to live a decent and peaceful life. In the face of these challenges militating against the Niger Delta woman's self-assertion and empowerment, one finds that she appears to be perpetually passive, powerless, and voiceless. These are the issues that have shaped the sensibilities of women in the area and which are crying out for literary attention.

Womanism: An African Alternative to Western Feminism

Contemporary female activism is associated with the successes achieved by feminist and women's empowerment movements that started in the eighteenth century with Mary Wollstonecraft's campaign for women's rights and suffrage. This phenomenon rapidly spread to other parts of America and Europe (Scott and Marshall, 2005: 218–220). The early days of feminist and women's liberation movements were championed by white women who vigorously pursued such ideals as equality of the sexes, female reproductive rights, access to education, and freedom in various spheres in which they were subordinated to their male counterparts in society. The feminist movement, over time, broke into different strands, amongst which are: radical feminism, bourgeois feminism, cultural feminism, Marxist feminism, and lesbian feminism (Evwierhoma, 2002: 41). The overriding principle guiding these feminist movements is the emancipation and empowerment of women across the world.

The issues and ideals pursued by proponents of these feminist movements have, in recent times, introduced a chasm between the more technologically advanced Western societies and those of the still developing societies. Scholars and feminist thinkers—like Jeanne-Marie Miller, Carole Boyce Davies, and Chioma Filomena Steady—have introduced issues of race and culture into the body of feminist theory (Evwerhoma, 2002: 46). These contemporary feminists are of the opinion that, because the earlier waves of feminism were championed by white women, the issues and challenges raised in their campaigns were peculiar to white women within the context of their own cultures, This invariably means that black women, who at that time were mostly slaves or menial workers in the homes of their white employers, were excluded.

One of these new wave feminist movements is known as "womanism", which adopts a theory that addresses the woman of African descent. Alice Walker first used the term "womanism" in 1983 to mean "a black feminist or feminist of colour". She used the term to describe African-American women's experiences. Womanists express the view that black women experience a different, more complex, form of oppression than white women, which requires that issues concerning her be scrutinised from a different perspective. Womanism is grounded in the African culture and it focuses on the unique experiences, struggles, needs, and desires of the African woman (Evwierhoma, 2002: 467).

The womanist theory encourages the humane nurturing of family values and cohesion of society at large. It is a direct opposition to the views of feminist thinkers like Nancy Chadrow, who—within the context of her Western culture—asserts that "the biological fact of childbearing is a key source of women oppression" (Scott and Marshall, 2005: 428–429). Such an assertion is not tenable to the womanist who places a premium on childbearing, positive male/female relationships, family values, and societal cohesion. African womanism is the springboard for Catherine Obianuju Acholonu's notion of "motherism", which supports the African woman's sensibilities, is not antagonistic to the African man, but rather challenges him to be aware of women's subjugation and to work towards alleviating them (Evwierhoma, 2002: 46).

Women's Struggle in the Niger Delta

Female activism in Nigeria is structured on the principles of African womanism and motherism. From the very beginning, female activists in Nigeria were not self-serving, but focused on the overall good of their society. Female activism is not a nouvelle experience in Nigeria. As far back as the colonial administration, women in Nigeria have resisted injustice and social inequity. The Aba Women's Riot of 1929 and the 1949 Egba Women's Riot led by Olufumilayo Ransome Kuti to protest against obnoxious colonial tax regimes in the then Western Region of Nigeria, are but two examples of women's activism in the early years of Nigeria's history.

Early mobilisation of women in the Niger Delta region was, and is still, largely shaped by environmental issues such as degradation and pollution caused by oil exploration activities of the oil companies, and fuelled by negligence on the part of these companies and government to the development needs of local communities. For instance, the Ogoni women of Rivers State rose up against the Anglo–Dutch multinational company, Shell, and succeeded in preventing it from returning to the facilities in their community in the 1990s. In 2002, women from Ugborodo in Delta State protested against the American multinational company, Chevron, and locked up their Escravos facility for ten days. In 2011, women of Gbaramatu in Bayelsa State also disrupted operations of Chevron at Chanomi Creek for several days. The demand of the various groups of women had been, and remains, the provision of basic infrastructure and social amenities for their communities.

Women's mobilisation at community levels is complemented by individual activists who believe that the people of the Niger Delta are not being accorded their rights or treated fairly by the multinationals and the government. Some of such Niger Delta female activists are: Ann Kio Briggs, Emem Okon, Sokari Ekine, and Stella Fyneface. These are women who have taken a stand in society to advocate not only for equality and the fair treatment of women in the Niger Delta, but who have also become champions of equity, justice, and good governance in Nigeria. They take their campaigns to the doorsteps of the individuals and institutions responsible for the injustices. They openly condemn acts and policies inimical to the growth, development, and wellbeing of the people. These female activists continue to demand justice and restitution for people of the Niger Delta region, and Nigeria at large.

Works of Emergent Niger Delta Dramatists

From its earliest origins, drama and theatre has been playing a vital role in the evolution of society. Drama serves as the uncensored watcher of society, and the dramatist, the watchman or woman whose duty is to hold up the reflection of their society via the mirror of their dramatic works. Every dramatist of every age feels the pulse of their society and faithfully re-creates the lives and events of their people for posterity. The Niger Delta region has, since independence, produced some notable dramatists, who—as social historians—have been watching and feeling the pulses of their society and have dutifully been using their works to realistically x-ray the state of their society.

Noted dramatists that originate from the region can be categorised into three distinct generations: the first, second, and third generations of Niger Delta playwrights. First generation Niger Delta playwrights would include: John Pepper Clark-Bekederemo, James Ene Henshaw, Simon Ambakederemo, Zulu Sofola, and Ola Rotimi. The second generation of Niger Delta playwrights would include: Sam Ukala, and Fred Agbeyegbe, while the third generation Niger Delta dramatists include: Barclays Ayakoroma, S. N. A. Agoro, Irene Salami, Effiong Johnson, and Matthew Umukoro.

The above categorisation of Niger Delta playwrights is premised thus: first generation writers are those who started writing in the wake of Nigeria's independence from British colonial rule. The themes of plays written in this era revolved mostly around nationhood and the crises of leadership and governance. Some examples of works written in this era are J. P. Clark's *The Raft*, Zulu Sofola's *King Emene* and Ola Rotimi's *The Gods are not to Blame*. The second and third generation Niger Delta playwrights are those who began writing from the 1980s into the new millennium. Writers of this period, in addition to issues of national concerns, embraced diverse subject matters in their works as they treated issues topical to their immediate and broader social environments.

As the twenty-first century unfurled, a new generation of playwrights emerged in the Nigerian dramatic terrain, popularly known as the new voices of Nigerian drama. In the Niger Delta dramatic scene, these new voices include: Stephen Inegbe, Best Ugula, Atakpo Uwemedimo, Dan Omatsola, Akpos Adesi, Kenneth Eni, and Ben Binebai. The thematic shift noticed in the writings of second and third generation Niger Delta dramatists becomes more entrenched in the works of the new voices in the region. These new breed of Niger Delta dramatists, aware of twenty-first century concerns, are responding to issues that reflect the wider global and Nigerian social contexts, as well as the ethnic societies they come from.

Synopsis of Selected Play Texts

This section looks at the portrayal of women in selected play texts emanating from the Niger Delta region. The play texts to be analysed include: Akpos Adesi's "Ebidein-ere" in *Agadagba Warriors and other Plays* (2008), Uwemedimo Atakpo's *Ken-Saro Wiwa-N-The Niger Delta Trial* (2006), Barclays Ayakoroma's *Dance on His Grave* (2005), Ben Binebai's *Beyond Nightmare* (2007), Irene Salami's *Emotan* (2001), and Bassey Ubong's *Zero-Sum Game* (2006).

Akpos Adesi's *Agadagba Warriors and Other Plays* dwell on the fundamental issues affecting the Niger Delta people and their terrain. The underlying tone of the plays suggests that only justice, fairness, respect for the rights of the people, and the development of the region can bring lasting peace to the region and nation at large. Adesi's *Ebidein-ere* eulogises the beautiful eponymous village belle who had been betrothed to Okirizi, the clan's champion, from birth. Drawing on the Trojan War theme, Esibiri—a warrior from Ossiama—abducts Ebidein-ere and the enraged Okirizi and warriors of his clan wage a battle against the people of Ossiama to rescue Ebidein-ere (Adesi, 2008: 36–37).

After her rescue from her abductors, Ebidein-ere declares that she no longer assents to the marriage between Okirizi and herself. The belle, who before her abduction had submissively accepted her imminent marriage to Okirizi, shocks the gathering of her kin in a sudden show of self-assertion, with the following declaration:

> I made a... vow to myself that come what may, I shall only stick to whomsoever that deflowers me. I love Okirizi no less but I cannot violate myself. (Adesi, 2008: 44)

Ebidein-ere's self-assertion is respected because Okirizi releases her from the engagement. The authoring of Ebidein-ere's character calls to question the intention behind the maiden's rescinding of her betrothal to Okirizi, the village champion, in favour of her abductor who, to all intents and purposes, dishonoured her before she was rescued.

Zero-Sum Game (2006), by Bassey Ubong, tells the story of Eton caught in the dilemma of either obeying tradition or obeying the dying wish of his father. The tradition of the land demands that where two deaths occur close to each other in a family, the corpse of the one who died first should be buried first. However, the circumstances surrounding the death of Eton's sister led him to abandon her corpse at the mortuary for a year. Eventually, while he was still trying to come to terms with her death and the decision to bury her, his father dies also, and with his dying breath directs that he be buried immediately after his death. Eton's wife, Toro, is portrayed as the typically voiceless and caring African wife who obeys every command of her husband. Her friend Dudu, on the other hand, is portrayed as a self-assertive character that confronts situations as they arise. Dudu and Eton's two sisters try to persuade Eton to do the right thing by burying his deceased sister before burying his father, but Eton rebuffs them. When the badgering became too much for Eton to take, he dismisses the women with: "Enough of this, all of you go behind and stay with my wife that is where women should be" (Ubong, 2006: 32–33). Against the dictates of tradition and various pleas to bury the sister first, Eton buries his father. However, as punishment for defying tradition, Eton eventually loses his own life.

Uwemedimo Atakpo's *Ken-Saro Wiwa-N-The Niger Delta Trial* (2006) x-rays the intrigues, the hardships, and the horrors that plague the region. It highlights the few who dare to challenge the perpetrators of the degradation and devastation going on in the region. *Ken-Saro Wiwa-N-The Niger Delta Trial* focuses on the heroic efforts of Ken-Saro Wiwa and his group of activist comrades, to effect positive change in the Niger Delta region. These Niger Delta activists ultimately pay with their lives for the Niger Delta struggle. The play has only one female character, Ms Anam Agoro, who ostensibly is merely a decorative piece in the fabric of the play. She is rendered voiceless for the larger part of the play, with her only remarkable quality being to raise solidarity songs in the face of life threatening situations.

Beyond Nightmare, written by Ben Binebai, is about three brave men who risk their lives to save Princess Tutu from the clutches of the "monster" that abducted her. When it is discovered that it was Ebeyein— the mother-general of the community, the only female member of the king's council of chiefs—who masterminded the abduction to dethrone the king (Ingobai) and usurp his throne, she is condemned to death and her position, the only female one in the council is abrogated. The queen and Chief Tonkepa speak up in condemnation of Ebeyein's actions, yet they plead that her life be spared (Binebai, 2007: 63). Eventually the king heeds the voice of reason, commutes Ebeyein death sentence and instead banishes her from the kingdom, and also restores the one female position in the council that was previously occupied by Ebeyein.

Analysis of Female Characters in the Plays

The plays discussed in the previous section of this chapter deal with issues ranging from leadership in society, cultural issues, and environmental and oil-related issues because most of them are located in Niger Delta communities. They also give considerable attention to issues that affect women and the challenges women face in their various communities on a daily basis. The disadvantages faced by women in patriarchal societies are evidenced in the works of these new generation writers from the region.

The cardinal patriarchal principle of women being "seen but not heard" is affirmed in Bassey Ubong's *Zero-Sum Game* (2006). The women in Eton's life attempt to reason with him, but because the "culture" of his society denies women the capacity for rational thinking, Eton refuses to listen to the advice and pleas of his wife, Toro, her friend, Dudu, and his sisters to obey the dictates of tradition and bury his sister before his father. Ms Anang in *Ken-Saro Wiwa-N-The Niger Delta Trial* adds nothing to the play apart from being the token representation of womanhood. In the face of the imminent death of the activists', Ms Anang's preoccupation, it seems, is raising solidarity songs instead of proactively championing the change that was needed. The presentation of the Ebidein-ere character in Adesi's *Ebidein-ere* re-affirms the patriarchal ideology of women as being irrational and senseless. She breaks off her engagement to Okirizi in order to give herself to the same abductor who had raped her in the false "cultural" belief that she has to stay committed to whoever it was that took her virginity. In the plays of the new generation Niger delta dramatists discussed here, Binebai's *Beyond Nightmare* is the only one which does not tow the line of the other writers in mirroring society's perception of Niger Delta women as being incapable of making meaningful contributions to important discourse. However, the character of Ebeyein, in *Beyond Nightmare,* is inevitably portrayed as an overly ambitious woman who aspires to overthrow Pere Ingobai in order to ascend the throne of the kingdom.

The portrayal of women in the plays considered above does not imbue them with positive qualities. These women are portrayed either as nitwits or schemers. However, plays such as Zulu Sofola's *Wedlock of the Gods* (1972), Irene Salami's *Emotan* (2001), and J.P. Clark's *The Wives Revolt* (2003) counter this approach to the representation of Niger Delta women. Even though *Wedlock of the Gods* was written as strands of new wave feminism were filtering into the African continent in the 1960s and 70s, Sofola, in her portrayal of Ogwoma, demonstrates the power of a woman's rights over her body. In the play Ogwoma refuses to sit in the ashes of mourning as tradition dictates for a woman whose husband dies and, rather, she reconciles with Uloko, her erstwhile lover. By presenting an independent Ogwoma, Sofola straddles both the old and the new. Ogwoma is seen to embrace the independence and freedom to do what she wants as her inalienable fundamental human right. But because the values of the old traditions are still very much alive in 1972, Ogwoma is made to pay for her "abominable" act.

Wedlock of the Gods foreshadows future writers advocating gender equality in their works. On the other hand, Irene Salami's *Emotan* embodies the African woman who takes pride in her 'womanity'. Writing from her unique perspective of a womanist, Salami portrays Emotan as a determined woman who sets out to restore justice in her community by dethroning Uwaifiokun, the usurper to the Benin throne, and enthroning the legitimate heir, Prince Ogun, as Oba Ewuare the Great of Benin Kingdom. Salami's works, like most other contemporary female writers in Nigeria, champions the cause of women's empowerment in Africa and provides positive female characters as role models.

The campaign for women empowerment is not championed by female writers alone, but by some male writers who continue to lend their voices to the struggle for gender equality. A case in point is J. P. Clark's *The Wives Revolt* which is a dramatic piece that shows women standing up to their menfolk to demand their rights. In the play, the women of Erhuwaren insist that the oil money paid to their community must be shared equally among the men and women of the community. When the men refuse to share the money equitably, the women stage a walkout on their men and refuse to undertake their "civic duties and responsibilities". Male writers like Clark challenge women to stand up and demand justice and equality for both sexes.

Conclusion

There are as yet, more male than female writers in the Niger Delta dramatic scene. Some of these male writers still perpetuate patriarchy through their depiction of female characters in their works. However, among the male dramatists, there are those who have realised that for the Niger Delta to become an egalitarian society, male and female members have to work positively together to effect the change needed. This group of writers, irrespective of their generation, are active in giving voice and power to their female characters.

The Niger Delta woman no longer waits passively for hand-outs from the male members of her society. She wants to be involved in the decision-making realm of her society, and she wants to be involved in the regeneration of her destroyed environments and in the development of her region and people. Education is no longer a barrier because uneducated women in local communities are mobilising and demanding their rights. Individually, new generation Niger Delta women are also asking questions, and they are taking their campaigns to the doorsteps of the perpetrators of injustice.

Even when the Niger Delta woman is branded a witch or mischief-maker, she no longer relents in her quest to achieve a just society. Emotan and Tamara—just like the contemporary Ann Kio Briggs, Emem Okon, Sokari Ekine, and others—are rising to challenge the structures of patriarchy and the ultimate subordination, victimisation, and underdevelopment of women in the region, and Nigeria at large.

The cultural, traditional, environmental, and physical challenges facing the Niger Delta woman in her community will be there for some time to come, but women in the region are beginning to challenge those structures that serve the purpose of keeping them on the fringes of social relevance. When the women of fictitious Erhuwaren and Toru-ama, like the women of Ugborodo, Gbaranmatu, Ogoni, and other Niger Delta communities, rise with one voice to demand justice, the perpetrators of injustice are compelled to listen to them and take action to address their demands. Niger Delta women are strong and determined, and if given the space, will perform creditably in any field of endeavour they participate in.

While the past is gone, the present and future are for the living to shape. Therefore, playwrights are expected to look beyond the myopic lens of patriarchy to realise that the only way to a truly egalitarian society is to ensure that everyone can aspire to be the best they can be without hindrance from man or culture, and without prejudice to sex. The emergence of female dramatists from the region is beginning to balance the scale with more and more plays being written for, and about, the Niger Delta woman. These emerging works are opening up new vistas of possibilities for women and providing them the opportunity to become relevant in society and to attain their full potential.

References

Adesi, A. (2008) "Ebideinere" *Agadagba Warriors and Other Plays*. Ilorin: NewArt.

Atakpo, U. (2006) *Ken-Saro Wiwa-N-The Niger Delta Trial*. Uyo: Modern Business Press.

Ayakoroma, B. (2005) *Dance on His Grave*. Yenagoa: Dee-Golfinger.

Bamidele, L. (2000) *Sociology of Literature*. Ibadan: Sterling Hodden.

Binebai, B. (2007) *Beyond Nightmare*. Ibadan: Kraft Books.

—. (2010) *When the Oil Runs Dry*. Yenagoa: Jebokab Limited.

Clark, J. P. (2003) *The Wives Revolt*, (Rev Ed.). Ibadan: University Press, Plc.

Evwierhoma, M. (2002) *Female Empowerment and Dramatic Creativity*. Ibadan: Caltop Publications.

Ibaba S. I. (2005) *Understanding the Niger Delta Crisis*. Port Harcourt: Amethyst Colleagues Publishers.

Salami, I. I. (2001) *Emotan*. Jos: Mazlink Nigeria.

Scott, J. and Marshal, G. (2005) *Oxford Dictionary of Sociology*. Oxford: OUP.

Sofola, Z. (1972) *Wedlock of the Gods*. Ibadan: Evans Brothers Limited.

Ubong, B. (2006) *Zero-Sum Game*. Uyo: Ivy Press.

CHAPTER EIGHT

THE SEMIOTICS OF CHURCH THEATRE: COMMUNITY, TRADITION, AND INNOVATION

GOWON AMA DOKI

Introduction

The 2009 International Conference of the African Theatre Association (AfTA) provided a platform for African theatre scholars to engage in intensive academic discourse on the theme: *New Directions in African Theatre and Performance.* This particular conference afforded participants the opportunity to engage in long overdue interrogation of new and emerging practices, critical approaches, pedagogies, and discourses on African theatre, performance, and related arts and media. It was at this forum that I first made public my notion of "show-off theatre" as a form of theatrical performance among the Tiv people of central Nigeria. However, like I observed even at that time, this form of theatre has always been in existence, and has only been made all the more popular and visible now, thus arousing my academic curiosity and interest.

In my first exploration of "show-off theatre" at that conference, I examined burial ceremony using the tenets of semiotics as critical parameters to unearth the meaning and contexts of the performance. The transformation which has changed Tiv burial practice from a simple cultural exercise to a complex social event involving large sums of money constituted the major thrust of this discussion. On conclusion, the study revealed that people engage in flamboyant spending basically to show how well placed and successful they are in society. The practice of sewing uniform costumes, hiring mourners, and constructing castles as graves— though not originally intended as theatre in the strictest sense of the word—could pass as a theatrical performance because of its communicative, as well as performative, attributes. The feedback I received at that conference inspired me to probe further into this new theatrical tradition or genre. Following from the above-mentioned insight, this study also attempts to look at yet another context where this type of theatricality manifests itself—the church.

The series of activities that could be described or analysed as performance that happen in the church space are too aesthetically and theoretically appealing to be ignored, at least not in the face of the renewed interest in new and emerging trends in theatre and performance practice. Within the context and realms of analysis in this chapter, it is most appropriate to first establish and conceptualise the church space, as well as the series of activities that take place in and around the church, as theatre. This would provide the needed framework and background for the ensuing analysis.

The Church Community, Tradition and Innovation

Contextually speaking, what distinguishes one church community from another is the approach and manner of conducting worship activities. These approaches constitute and manifest as the traditions of the various church communities. Such traditions account for why people belong to different church communities. The extent of an individual's attraction to a particular church community depends largely on the impression and sense of belonging that they get from the specific community. Children most often are born into certain church communities. As a result of their parents' affiliation to a particular church denomination, they live, grow up and function as members of that community until they are mature enough to determine their own affiliations.

Churches all over the world experience change at some point in their respective histories. It may either be a change in their activity profile or in their institutional or administrative structures. New converts, widely travelled members, or members in the diaspora are among the various agents of change in the church. It is this change that is regarded here as innovation. New ideas are introduced usually to moderate or modify old ways of doing things when thought necessary by the aforementioned agents.

Under examination here is the Catholic Church, whose activities, are contextualised in this work as a series of episodic performances—the summation of which could pass as theatre. Several other church denominations, including the pentecostal churches, also employ a wide range of theatricality in their services. Nevertheless, as a practising catholic, I am more conversant with what happens in the Catholic Church and will draw my examples from there.

Theatre and Performance

The evolution of theatre is rooted in the ontology and cosmology of a people living together within a geographical or geo-political location. Their total existence is therefore predicated on their social, economic, political, and religious worldviews and beliefs. Theatrical performances by such a group of people would usually reflect their way of being and living in the world. Such a people must be familiar with the objects and themes of their communal performances—only then would theatre, according to Marsh Cassady (1992: 3), live up to its criterion of attracting people and sustaining their interest. For the purpose of this chapter, I will consider any spectacle that is well-structured and presented before an audience for the purpose of entertainment, education, orientation, information, or conscientisation as theatrical performance. This would naturally include activities that take place within the church space, which is conceptualised in this work as theatre. To support this claim, Hameed Olutoba Lawal's views on the scope of theatre would help. According to Lawal, "Theatre is not inherent in drama only rather it encompasses the words and actions of our everyday activities" (2010: 1). This is, perhaps, another confirmation of the church space as theatre and its beehive of activities as performance.

According to Antoine Leporc (2011), Erving Goffman came up with what he called dramaturgical theory, in which he argues that:

> Communication is primarily a performance. In our everyday life, we are mere actors playing a role... He further emphasized the idea of front and back stage in which we respectively standardised and normalised our behaviour for public observation as well as controlling the information we give about ourselves in such a way as to convince the audience, and a place with less public space in which performers are present but audience is not, and the performers can step out of character without fear of disrupting the performance.

Leporc's reading of Goffman further amplifies the position that what we say or do not say to others constitutes performance—from shuffling ideas and options, to sleeping and waking up. Welsh argues that, "Goffman's theory was designed for what he calls "total institutions" and that theories should not be applied where they have not been tested." According to Welsh:

> The dramaturgy theory should only be applied in cases that involve people associated with a "total institution" or in other words an institution where all individuals are subordinated to and dependent upon an authority

(colleges, prisons, monasteries or orphanages). (Welsh 1990 cited in Leporc, 2011)

This position by Welsh gives credence to my choice of the church space as a case study. On virtually all fronts, members of a church congregation are subordinated. First to the scripture, then to the church doctrine, and on the primary scene, the priest who is a representative of the bishop, who is a representative of the pope as a local ordinary, and then the pope who is regarded by the Church as God's representative here on earth. A cursory look at the above would quite comfortably situate my discussion on the church space within the framework of the dramaturgical theory. Institutionally, therefore, the interaction of parties in this context is basically performative. For anyone to achieve salvation, which is the ultimate desire of every member of the congregation, you must be seen to perform not only the rites of worship but also demonstrate some observable feats of true Christianity.

Performance ethnography is another frame that offers a relevant context for interrogating emerging or non-theorised performance forms across the globe. It encourages a participatory engagement between performers and their audience as both parties mutually engage in the examination of issues in performance. In the abstract to her article on performance ethnography, Oberg (2008: 1) observes that:

> Performance ethnography, an emerging arts based methods of qualitative inquiry, presents a tangible opportunity to bridge the gap between scholarly activity and teaching and learning. ...performance ethnography transforms the theatre from a place of entertainment to avenue for participatory action research that extends beyond the performance itself.

In furtherance of her argument, Oberg goes on to observe that:

> Through re-enacted performance the oppression of socially imposed roles is unveiled on stage and examined by both audience and actors simultaneously, thereby enabling a transformative critique of values, attitudes and practices. (Oberg, 2008: 1)

Reasoning deductively in this instance, one would in like manner opine that, through the re-enactment of the life and times of Christ by the priest, the congregation is brought together in communion, where each member reflects on his or her life. This reflection is actually a mental critique of how well or not one has kept the values, beliefs, doctrines, and practices of the church as is expected of them. Performance ethnography therefore functions as a catalyst for self-examination, evaluation, and fellowship.

While Goffman's theory of dramaturgy is useful in re-affirming my claim that the church and its activities constitutes theatre, Oberg's theory of performance ethnography assists in my attempt to appropriate the re-enactment by the priest and the understanding, assimilation, response, and self-examination by the audience (congregation) as performance. Akin to the above theoretical postulations by Goffman and Oberg, a critical examination of the church space, herein referred to as *Church Theatre,* will be attempted using the instrument of signs and signification borrowed from semiotics.

The Semiotics of a Church Theatre

Semiotics, simply put, is the science of signs and signification. It involves the relationship between a sign, an object, and a meaning. It is concerned with the production and interpretation of meaning. Morris (1964: 1) identifies three factors that guide interpretation:

1. The descriptive aspects which directs the interpreter to a particular object.
2. The appraise aspects which highlights object qualities enabling evaluation.
3. The prescriptive aspects which directs one to respond in specific ways.

Semiotics as a concept can be approached on three fronts: icon, index and symbols. However, of these three, the symbol as an instrument of thought—which allows a person to think about something apart from its immediate presence—is most suitable in a discussion such as this. Danesi, while discussing the primary essence of semiotics, opines that: "The primary task of semiotics is to identify, document and classify the main types of signs and how they are used in representational activities" (2004: 24). This chapter, thus, examines the series of activities in the church which qualifies as performance and, thus, theatre. The primary task, therefore, is to identify the signs in these performances and show how they aid communication and interpretation. Ultimately, therefore, the representational capacity of the sign in performance is the focus of this study.

Predominantly, the Catholic Church thrives on symbols. The crucifix, the bells, the candles, the positioning and colour decoration of the altar during mass, as well as the colour of the chasuble worn by the priest during mass are all agents of symbolic representation in the Catholic Church. The architectural design of the church with a thrust or proscenium stage, an auditorium for the congregation (audience), and the stage properties adorning the altar (stage) could pass for a theatre venue. In setting the stage, some churches employ aesthetic balancing by placing the crucifix on one side and the Maryann statue on the other.

The chasuble is the garment worn by a priest during the mass celebration. The colour of the chasuble reflects the season of the church's calendar. The audience or congregation identifies with this as they appreciate, understand, and remind themselves of the time and mood of celebration on sighting the priest and the colour of his chasuble. Green, for instance, symbolises the "freshness of God", white symbolises "hope", purple "repentance", red "the shedding of blood", and gold symbolises "the glory of God". All these provide a deeper engagement with the congregation beyond the ordinary colours that are seen. Each season in the church calendar requires specific behaviour and activity from members of the church, and the colour of the chasuble serves as a point of reference for the congregation. The colour of chasuble could, therefore, be said to be a prescriptive aspect of the sign that guides interpretation in the church. It directs the congregation to the season and what is required of them for that particular season.

As part of the costume, the chasuble defines the priest as a protagonist character in the drama of celebrating mass. Mass servants, who also adorn the altar as support characters, re-inforce the character of the priest by wearing costumes that differentiate them from the rest of the congregation. Though no specific type of costume is required of congregation members, people usually aspire to come "clean and neat" to the Lord, which explains why members usually try to look their best as they come to the church in worship of the Lord. The spectacle here is the defining role of various costumes during the service, and how such costumes—in a representative capacity—elevate the psyche of the congregation, and thus accentuate their faith and worship.

Another point of semiotic interest is the re-enactment by the priest of the life and times of Christ. The priest, herein also referred to as the protagonist, is the central character around which the drama of mass celebration revolves. He is re-inforced on either side of the stage by altar boys or mass servants who usually assist him in playing his role. In this theatre, the audience or congregation, just as in conventional theatre, appreciates the protagonist (priest) more when he is vibrant, mobile, and articulate. Like the theory of the fourth wall, both the actors and the audience engage in a communal experience, as though they are in the real world of Christ and his disciples. Thus, the re-enactment of the life and times of Christ by the priest during mass, where in a routine fashion the priest consecrates bread and blood before administering communion, is an appraisive sign which enables the church—through the instrumentality of performance—to highlight the qualities of Christ for a possible self-evaluation by the audience or congregation.

Music and dance complete the semiotic cycle of a church theatre. Like in Greek mythology, the choir as a part of the wider audience serves as the chorus or orchestra. Songs are selected and rehearsed for presentation on the day of production (usually on Sundays). As total theatre, the songs (hymns), the script (Bible), message (preaching) and costume (chasuble) must be in harmony with the season on the church's calendar. Any deviation from the norm would attract a reaction from the audience or congregation who are conversant with the signs and meanings of the performance. The songs are carefully selected to help put the audience into the proper mood and perspective for worship, and also to enhance their assimilation of the message.

The collection of alms during the offertory is another signifier that aids interpretation and assessment of the priest's performance. The performance of the priest, both on stage and back stage, where he occasionally steps out of character, usually influences the size of the offertory. A "good performance" (a priest who preaches well and sings or says the mass compellingly) is likely to attract a far more generous contribution from the congregation than a "bad performer" (a priest who is regarded as boring or uninspiring). The size of the collection during offertory, when audited over a period of time, could attest to the "performance" of the priest in charge. Sometimes, the congregation could withhold their financial support or giving during the offertory in protest against the continued stay of a particular priest whom they no longer want in their parish.

Broadly speaking, therefore, symbolic agents such as the crucifix, bells, candles, stage setting, colour of chasuble, architectural design of the church, acting, music and dance, as well as the offertory collection are all signposts or objects of signification in the church theatre. Collectively, these agents of semiotic relevance add up to enhance the understanding and interpretation of messages in the church.

Conclusion

This chapter, by thoroughly examining the operational paraphernalia of the Catholic Church mass, has attempted to show how a church service can be conceptualised as theatre. Scholars and practitioners of the theatre are encouraged to take more than a passing interest in this type of theatre. This will enable them not only to theorise, but also extract from its vast traditions certain aspects and best practices that could help revitalise live theatre performance. In Nigeria for instance, live theatre is no longer as viable as it used to be, and the usual reason given by practitioners is that of the low patronage by audiences. Interestingly, however, it can be observed that church attendance in Nigeria has continued to grow, which implies that something must be right about the conduct and practice of this brand of theatre that could be explored by practitioners of conventional live theatre.

For instance, whereas conventional live theatre charges its audience gate takings, the church allows the audience to give their contribution as offerings as they are led to do. Managers of conventional live theatre performances could also adopt this approach by allowing people to watch a performance and in-between the performance announce their support or donation to the company as they are moved by the enjoyment of the performance. This is in line with Baz Kershaw's assumption that "performance can be most usefully described as an *ideological transaction* between a company of performers and the community of their audience" (1992: 16 *original emphasis*). In furtherance of this argument, Kershaw infers that:

> Ideology is the source of the collective ability of performers and audience to make more or less common sense of the signs used in performance, the means by which the aims and intentions of theatre companies connect with the responses and interpretations of their audiences. Thus, ideology provides the framework within which companies encode and audiences decode the signifiers of performance. I view performance as a transaction because, evidently, communication in performance is not simply uni-directional, from actors to audience. The totally passive audience is a figment of the imagination, a practical impossibility; and, as any actor will tell you, the reactions of audiences influence the nature of a performance.

This intrinsic connection between the performer and the audience requires of managers of this kind of theatre, a deeper understanding of the psychology, philosophy, and mind-set of the persons and places involved. In contemporary Nigerian society, for instance, people usually cherish personal recognition where all attention is focused on them. At such times when they have everyone's attention, they become what Augusto Boal refers to as "spect-actors", and as performers in their own right they are more likely to contribute generously to the finances of the theatre company.

Evidently, notions of performance encompasses all aspects of life, and by examining the church space and its various activities through a semiotic lense, this chapter seeks to open up a vista of scholarly debate around such performative traditions and vestiges of performance in contemporary society.

References

Alexander, B. K. (2005) "Performance Ethnography. The Re-enacting and Inciting of Culture." *The Sage Handbook of Qualitative Research,* 3rd Edition. Eds. N. K. Denzin and V. S. Lincoln. Thousand Oaks, CA: Sage.

Cassady, M. (1992) *The Theatre and You: A Beginning.* Colorado: Meriwether Publishing Ltd.

Danesi, M. (2004) *Messages, Signs and Meanings: A Basic Textbook in Semiotics and Communication Theory.* 3rd Edition. Toronto: Canadian Scholar's Press Inc.

Denzini, N. K. (2003) *Performance Ethnography: Critical Pedagogy and the Politics of Culture.* Thousand Oaks, CA: Sage.

Kershaw, B. (1992) *The Politics of Performance: Radical Theatre as Cultural Intervention.* London: Routledge.

Lawal, O. (2010) *Fundamentals of Theatre Arts.* Ibadan: Glory and Land Publishing Company.

Leporc, A. (2011) "Interpretation of Erving Goffman's Dramaturgical Theory in Relation to the 'Online Stage' and Facebook." [Online] Available at: <http://antoineleporc.com/interpretation-erving-goffman's-dramaturgical-theory-relation-"online-stage"-facebook/> (Accessed 23 April 2011).

Morris, C. W. (1964) *Signification and Significance: A Study of the Relation of Signs and Values.* Cambridge, Massachusetts: MIT Press.

Oberg, C.M. (2008) "Performance Ethnography: Scholarly Inquiry in the Here and Now." *Transformative Dialogues: Teaching & Learning Journal* 2(1). [Online] Available at: <http://kwantlen.ca/TD/TD.2.1/TD.2.1_Oberg_Performance_Ethnography.pdf> (Accessed 23 April 2011).

Shakespeare, W. (1957) "As you." *The Oxford Shakespeare: The Complete Works,* 2nd Edition. Eds. S. Wells and G. Taylor. New York: Oxford University Press.

CHAPTER NINE

IN SEARCH OF HIDDEN THEATRE

JOHAN ESTERHUIZEN

Introduction

There are many descriptions of theatrical forms: from Artaud we get the "theatre of cruelty", there is Peter Brook's deadly, holy, rough, and immediate theatre as described in *The Empty Space* (1968), Grotowski's *poor theatre*, and the image, invisible, and forum theatre described by Augusto Boal in his seminal *Theatre of the Oppressed* (1979). In South Africa, Rolf Solberg categorised alternative theatrical activity as: majority theatre, committed theatre, contestatory theatre, and community theatre, amongst others (and there are many more to choose from). We all wish to capture the term that best describes what we experience theatrically. However, it is not always the case that the practitioners of a given category necessarily agree with or painstakingly abide by the definition hoisted upon them!

What I have experienced over the past six years, during my involvement with the Buya Schools Theatre Festival in Stellenbosch, South Africa, is theatre that is hidden for the most part from the general suburban public. It is not a theatre that is readily available by going on one of Sam's "Township Cultural Tours". It is not "on tap", as it were, and will not be found by checking the "What's On" column in *The Atlantic Sun*—a local newspaper distributed in the Western Cape Province of South Africa. In other words, Buya Schools Theatre Festival has a minimum amount of publicity or hype attached to it. It is just that: Hidden Theatre.

How then do we navigate the labyrinth? Where then are we to look and what is it we will discover? I can only answer these questions by describing my own journey, the journey of an *ouerige oomie* (old gent) with a love for all things theatrical.

Discovering the Hidden Theatre

My particular road to discovery started in 2005 when a young IsiXhosa speaking fellow, with an equal love for all things theatrical, approached me as the then director of the University of Stellenbosch's H. B. Thom Theatre to host a schools' theatre festival. His name is Given Jikwana, founder of the Black Adventist Performance Academy (BAPA). The name of his proposed festival was the Buya Festival—"buya" means "come" in IsiXhosa. The festival would be aimed at high and primary schools drawn from Khayelitsha, a vast, sprawling suburb of Cape Town. This is an area lacking in conventional theatre facilities, but, as I was soon to find out, certainly not lacking in theatrical tradition and overwhelmingly talented performers.

The first festival was scheduled for May 2006, prior to which we arranged a day-long workshop in the H.B. Thom Theatre where skills transfer—both artistically and in terms of getting to know the technical aspects of the theatre—were paramount. As fate would ordain, this workshop took place during Athol Fugard's visit to Stellenbosch and he willingly spent an hour describing the methods employed by the Serpent Players in constructing their inspirational plays. Was this Garage Theatre meeting Hidden Theatre? In any event, Fugard's inspirational words led us to determine that the following year would include a writers' workshop before schools started compiling their scripts. Some fifteen schools participated in the first of our Buya Festivals, and the figure now stands at twenty-five schools. My immediate impression was: astonishment at the range of themes; admiration for the ingenuity, enthusiasm, and creative flair; and amazement at the sheer logistics that needed to be overcome in presenting these performances.

In the second year of the festival, our first writers' workshop was conducted by two remarkable theatre-makers, Themba Lonzi and Fatima Dike. They inspired a belief in the young Buya participants in the value and dramatic potential of their stories. The common themes not unknown to Themba or Fatima due to their experiences of the rigours of Township life. Nor were the characters that commonly populate the plays concealed from their vision, but sharply edged and breathing life. So the threads of gangsterism and rape, of poverty and HIV/AIDS, of a history of poor education and political turmoil, and of democracy and xenophobia that ran through *my* Hidden Theatre were as actual to *them* as Macbeth's lust for ambition was to me. My journey had indeed begun and it became clear I was the one whose eyes needed opening.

A period of study leave provided me with the opportunity to, metaphorically speaking, stare Township life squarely in the eye. It was an opportunity to travel the Mew Ways and Spine Roads of our city, to get to know Nyanga as *Sakkiesdorp* and to find a tavern or three providing the ideal meal for 22.00 South African Rands (about £1.36 British Pounds)—with a drink included. And, if you are after a take-away meal, you do not have to look any further than Landsdowne Road's famous braai corner, where you can buy your meat off a blazing brazier cum grill—and according to your clan affiliation.

Figure 9-1: Buya Festival 2008. Learners from Harry Gwala High School

By 2009, we had extended the Buya Festival to include a number of Townships such as Bloekombos, Drift Sands and Mfuleni, Blue Downs, and Kraaifontein, and along with my young mentor and guide, Given Jikwana, we criss-crossed the Cape Flats. If theatre holds up a mirror unto nature, I was forced to ponder on the reflection. The sheer volume of houses, the busyness of people getting on with their lives in conditions of shocking deprivation, and the sense of being in "pot-hole" Africa where the "cockroach taxis rule" became not the aghast exception but the familiar rule. At night travelling the Old Faure Road after a visit to Mfuleni, I was introduced to the surreal image of the ladies of the night plying their trade alongside braziers that lit up the avenue of tall wattle trees in glowing orange hues—not two or three such pyres, but ten or fifteen such beckons to life on poverty road.

And everywhere poverty! Turn off here, left there, right then right again avoiding the jay-walkers, the dogs, and always... the pot-holes in the roads. Until you arrive at the schools—schools with names of hope and aspiration. Schools with names such as: *Thembelihle* (Beautiful Hope) and *Dalubuhle* (Create Beauty), *Masibambisane* (Let's Work Together) and *Masibambane* (Let's Be Together), and my particular favourite, *Sizimisele*

(We are Determined)—protected from gangs by the *Bambanani* anti-crime volunteers and rusty barbed wire fences. Outside the gates, waiting for break time, were the Mamas waiting to sell their wares to the hungry school children, who are often set a-drooling by the delicious aroma of food being prepared in the staffrooms, ready to be handed out to those youngsters who would be given their only meal for the day. Class monitors standing in line for the loaves of bread that accompany the soup, samp, or lentil dish that awaits them.

I remember being introduced to Miss Thandi, the tall, imposing, and very attractive Head of Department of Arts and Culture at Luhlaza High. "Did I know Luhlaza was the first high school in Khayelitsha, founded in '85—a school with a strong tradition and proud of their history in the struggle?" she asks. "No," I tell her, "I'm only just finding out." Then it is on to Matthew Goniwe High, where a Zimbabwean teacher—Stanley Mutetwa—leads the gifted and committed drama club. Next up it is the irrepressible deputy head of Intshayelelo Primary, Mr Mbobo, who takes multi-tasking to amazing heights—he takes lunch, staff meetings, and rehearsals all at the same time. Always on the move, and always determined to give his learners the optimum opportunities available to them, whether it is netball, soccer, choir competitions or drama—and the school display cabinet has the glittering awards to prove it.

Figure 9-2: Buya Festival 2011: Members of the Makukhanye Youth Theatre Group

My search continued to be a revelation, and with each trip a new experience, with new people to meet and—most importantly—a new rehearsal and a new piece of theatre to watch. And so I began to recognise the aesthetics of this Hidden Theatre. In a flash, desks are piled into a corner, a drum appears, voices lusty and true burst forth—"let the show begin". The Hidden Theatre is right there, tangible, filled with an energy and collective insight that has to be seen and experienced to be understood. Silhouetted images of a class ganging up on a newly arrived Democratic Republic of the Congo (DRC) child; a schoolgirl's rape and her spiritual recovery; the fun and unashamed comedy extracted from the corner preacher; a fake *sangoma*, the con job on rural folk who are not aware of devious city ways; taverns that come alive to the strains of Township jive; and the biting satire of *The Three Rats*—H, I, and V.

The stories are endlessly creative and the style of theatre minimalistic, physical, and bridged with drumming, song, and dance. The content largely reflects the circumstance of the young people's lives. The work is always well rehearsed, and in five years I have seen only one under-prepared presentation. Some of the work is finely choreographed, some more loosely blocked—leaving ample space for improvisation and reactive staging. The choral work is of a very high standard, both in the primary and high school sections.

One of the greatest problems, and maybe why so much Hidden Theatre remains unnoticed, is the lack of formal, fully written scripts. A play is rarely repeated—you only get a few months whilst the group are together to see it and that is that. This could be ascribed to the oral nature of traditional *Nguni* drama, but also to the fact that the work is so closely woven together by the participants, that they feel no need to carry a script into rehearsal. The text is improvised and often retains marvellous moments of spontaneous ad hoc dialogue that can suddenly burst forth from an actor's character. But the work is virtually never undisciplined, sloppy, or half-baked, and the rehearsal and performance are approached with full concentration—the underlying sentiment is that "you just do not let the team down". I have seen rehearsals become pretty heated and unpleasant should one of the actors muck about or fail to give of their best. Usually, in such cases, when next you see the play you would find the said actor is no longer in the group. And although there is a lot of competition for the lead roles, once the group have decided on the casting everyone either gets on with the work or gets out of the group. This is because group dynamic is an essential and binding element in Hidden Theatre.

Seen in the context of the African aesthetic, however, this should not come as a surprise. In the introduction to Kofi Agawu's excellent article, "The Communal Ethos in African Performance", he comments:

> In many traditional African societies, practically every domain of performance is conditioned by a desire on the part of participants to join rather than divide, to bring together rather than set apart, to unify rather

than splinter—in short a communal ethos. "I am because I belong with others." (Agawu, 2007: 1)

As a personal experience, my search has proven to be both a revelation and an initiation. The opportunity to take the turn-off and become acquainted with the texture of Township tastes, smells, sights, and sounds has been profound and invigorating. Those textures that are often harshly, sometimes comically, portrayed in Hidden Theatre—the melting pot of a vibrant society wracked with poverty but which displays such a resilience and determination to seek alternative expression beyond their immediate circumstances. My advice to the theatre loving public is to get out there and discover the theatrical treasure that is the rich world of this Hidden Theatre. You will not be disappointed!

Note

1. To view associated videos of the performances discussed in this chapter, use the following YouTube links:

   Part 1: <http://youtu.be/JyckX-VHI4w> or search for "In search of hidden theatre—Part 1"
   Part 2: <http://youtu.be/sWO3tEVjjVA> or search for "In search of hidden theatre—Part 2"
   Part 3: <http://youtu.be/f3_6a2q5kPo> or search for "In search of hidden theatre—Part 3"

   Note that these YouTube links were functional at the time of publishing, and that no responsibility is accepted for any future problem with accessing the material.

References

Agawu, K. (2007) *The Communal Ethos in African Performance: Ritual, Narrative and Music Among the Northern Ewe.* Barcelona: TransRevista Transcultural de Musica, julio, numero 011.
Boal, A. (1979) *The Theatre of the Oppressed.* London: Routledge.
Brook, P. (1968) *The Empty Space.* New York: Atheneum.

CHAPTER TEN

ZEF/POOR WHITE KITSCH CHIQUE: SOUTH AFRICAN COMEDIES OF DEGRADATION[1]

ANTON KRUEGER

Introduction: Enter the Ninja

> I represent South African culture... a lot of different things... blacks, whites, coloureds, English, Afrikaans, Xhosa, Zulu – *watookal*.[2] I'm like... all these different people, fucked into one person...
> —Tudor Watkins Jones, aka "Ninja"[3]

Ninja, who fronts the freak hip hop band Die Antwoord, might not be quite what Desmond Tutu had in mind when he described South Africans as the "Rainbow People of God",[4] a happy harmonious amalgamation of different races. In his introduction to their seminal comic track, "Enter the Ninja", Ninja presents himself as a mongrel gutter dog, both embracing and parodying a syncretic fusion of the many different cultures and races of South Africa—celebrating as well as subverting the rainbow nation discourse. As he said in an interview with South Africa's *News24*: "South African culture is quite a fucking fruit salad... a fucking fucked rainbow nation. South Africa's totally fucked... but in a cool way"[5]. The cool side of being "fucked" in this way is *Zef*.

Zef denotes a particular style of vulgar[6] humour which has been emerging more and more in South Africa during the past decade. It involves a way of presenting a persona in a purposefully degrading way, exaggerating one's appearance and mannerisms as low class, ill-bred, and boorish. This chapter sets out to consider the recent popularity of *Zef* and examine its connection, specifically, to popular Afrikaans folk rock culture, a lineage of white poverty, and the disgrace experienced by many white Afrikaner people after apartheid.

Revolutions in Afrikaner Identity

1989 was a watershed year in South Africa. Amidst growing unrest, President P. W. Botha was asked to resign by the National Party and F. W. de Klerk became acting president. The following year, de Klerk unbanned the African National Congress (ANC) and prepared for the release of Nelson Mandela and the dismantling of apartheid. In white Afrikaner culture it was a time of uprising and rebellion by young Afrikaners who did not want to be conscripted into the then on-going border wars[7] or used as fodder to quell upheavals in the townships. This was a generation of white men who would have preferred to spend their gap-year working in pubs in the United Kingdom while watching the Springboks play rugby against New Zealand, rather than being forced to fight.

Also, following the end of apartheid in 1994 much that was formerly celebrated as part of the Afrikaner heritage came to be publically portrayed as shameful. For example, one of the major Afrikaner holidays during the National Party rule was the Day of the Covenant, which celebrated the victory of a small group of pioneering *Voortrekkers*[8] over a Zulu army numbering more than ten thousand. Today, the holiday has been renamed "Reconciliation Day" and the memorial at the site of the battle mourns the loss of the three thousand Zulu warriors who died in the battle.

Similarly, Mads Vestergaard points out that some of the many symbols have been changed or reinterpreted in the new dispensation:

> The national anthem was an Afrikaner anthem; the flag was an Afrikaner flag. The streets were named after heroes from nationalist Afrikaner history, and airports and dams bore the names of Afrikaner politicians. (2011: 24)

All of these have changed since 1994. The inheritance of the present generation of Afrikaners, then, is largely one of shame. During apartheid, there was a sense of shame inculcated by the accusations from the international community; and after the fall of apartheid there has been a rising sense of disgrace in the eyes of the new dispensation, who have rewritten perspectives on South Africa's history. For example, members of the ANC's military wing, *Umkhonto we Sizwe*—who were formerly referred to as "terrorists"—entered parliament as "freedom fighters"; and staunch National Party leaders who had previously been represented as bastions of moral law and order became redefined as callous war mongers. Perhaps this sense of shame experienced by young Afrikaners in the face of reversals to their political power, since the end of apartheid, has been permitted an outlet in the embrace of the vulgarity embodied by *Zef.*

Afrikaans musicians have long been at the forefront of challenging norms about power relations in South Africa. In his essay "Re-thinking Whiteness", Christopher Ballantine writes that:

> white musicians [in South Africa] have stressed the need for self-reinvention in music that is ironic, unpredictable, transgressive. These songs play with malleable identities; tokens of disdain for fixed or essential identities, they are hopeful signposts towards a more integrated future. (2004: 105)

Popular folk and rock music play a key role in representing and effecting the transformation of a generation of Afrikaans youth. At the end of the 1980s, for example, an alternative Afrikaans movement in popular music was founded on its opposition to the status quo. It became known as the *Voëlvry*[9] movement, with artists such as Johannes Kerkorrel, Bernaldus Niemand, and Koos Kombuis defying the strict Calvinism which defined the older generation. They sang against military conscription, against the oppression of black South Africans, and against hypocrisy in general.

The end of apartheid in 1994 signalled a victory for the aims of this movement, and yet it also meant that these musicians lost much of their revolutionary impetus. A number of them died tragically, such as Kerkorrel (by suicide) and Niemand (in a drink-driving accident), while Koos Kombuis settled into a "comfortable" role as author and father. Kombuis is no longer the firebrand he once was, and now identifies more easily with the middle-aged followers he first attracted in his youth during the 1980s, rather than the new generation of young Afrikaners. Kombuis has been identified by some as one of the first to position himself as being *Zef,*[10] although he no longer openly associates himself with the ethos of the new *Zef* musicians. Their use of *Zef* as a style of musical performance has also constituted a revolution of sorts—but this is an *apolitical* uprising. Although its mode can sometimes come across as *faux* anger, it is generally more comic and self-denigrating than *Voëlvry* ever was.

In this chapter, I would like to consider how *Zef* has associated itself particularly with poor whites and a heritage of shame, following the political changes of 1994 and their impact on the Afrikaner people. For the purposes of this chapter, "Afrikaner" refers specifically to the ethnic, white culture[11] forged by the Great Trek (1835–1846) and reinforced by the two Boer wars against the British (1880–1881 and 1899–1902).[12] As Mads Vestergaard points out, the white ethnic category of Afrikaner includes both heterodox and orthodox movements (2011: 19), which have either resisted or reinforced the established values of a group referred to by David Harrison in the title of his book as *The White Tribe of Africa* (1986).

Although this cultural group has come to be associated with racism—since they institutionalised apartheid—and the Calvinistic conservatism of their religion—in terms of their founding of the *Nederduitse Gereformeerde Kerk*[13]—it is important to bear in mind that many white Afrikaner people see the origins of their ethnicity in a desire for freedom from oppression by the imperial British and a desire for self-rule, rather than locating it in a desire to dominate other races. As Melissa Steyn points out:

> The self-esteem, indeed the very self-image, of Afrikaner nationhood was forged within a mythology that celebrated the courage of a people who refused to be subordinated to the British Empire. (2004: 147)

The nationalist Afrikaner government that came into power in 1948 overtly reinforced an ethnic Afrikaner identity. When the National Party were finally defeated in 1994, after ruling uninterruptedly for 46 years, this implied—for many ethnic Afrikaners—defeat, failure, guilt, and self-abnegation. Steyn notes that "For Afrikaners—whatever the ethical issues may be—the end of the Old South Africa cannot but be accompanied by feelings of loss" (2004: 150), and Vestergaard points out that in the new dispensation "white Afrikaners must live with a host of new uncertainties" (2011: 19).

The advent of democracy also signalled the beginning of encroaching poverty for a number of whites who had previously been protected by the state via programs designed for their upliftment. Some had previously been employed by the civil service of the apartheid government which had centralised agriculture, mining, telecommunications, and transport, and they suddenly found themselves unemployed when these services became privatised under the new dispensation. This has led to destitution among the white population for around ten per cent of their total population of approximately 450,000 people—a statistic which continues to increase yearly (Reuters, 2010).

This legacy of poor white Afrikaners can be traced all the way back to the British concentration camps of the Boer War. Lord Kitchener's "scorched earth" policy razed countless Boer farms to the ground and after this period, "a lengthy rural crisis and rapid industrialization turned many Afrikaners from farmers into an impoverished urban proletariat" (Vestergaard, 2001: 21).[14] Affirmative action programs for Afrikaners, instituted by the National Party government, helped to alleviate poor white

Afrikaner poverty by employing many as civil servants and creating special funds for education, as well as by giving them preferential treatment when awarding business contracts (Vestergaard, 2001). With the end of apartheid, Afrikaners lost their privileged position not only amongst the general population of the country, but amongst the white population itself.

Many poor white Afrikaners in post-apartheid South Africa became associated with *Zef*, which was originally a derogatory term used to describe unemployed (or blue collar) poor whites living in caravan parks.[15] The term originated in the 1950s and 60s to deride a working class driving "souped up" Ford Zephyrs with flash wings (Du Preez, 2011: 102). It was first used as an insult to refer to the kitsch tastes of unrefined people, much like the American term "redneck". More recently, the portrayal of *Zef* has become a staple feature of a number of comedy shows in South Africa. However, there seems to be more to this development than mockery, since the new designation of *Zef* also implies an attitude of resilience. This new designation is linked to notions of authenticity, and to a kind of rudeness which implies a sign of health—as in the idiomatic expression, "to be in rude health". First used to ridicule an underclass for being unsophisticated, the word has now been reclaimed as a marker of authenticity. This is an authenticity tied to cultural origins, to a sense of community fostered by those unable or unwilling to move very far away from the neighbourhood in which they were born. It locates the authentic in myths of origin, and a sense of being rooted in the past.

The idea of "being *Zef*" has, then, been around for decades in South Africa, but it has only recently been introduced to the rest of the world as a peculiarly South African phenomenon. The term was recently popularised by Die Antwoord, a mock hip-hop outfit, who became an overnight sensation when their YouTube clip "Enter the Ninja" (stewartridgway, 2010a) shot to ten million views in just a few days. Within a month, their website had attracted 41 million hits (SABC 3, 2010), securing them a world tour and recording contract with the international label Interscope.

With their mullet haircuts, Ninja's amateur tattoos and language peppered with a stream of vulgarities such as *naai, poes, fok, kont*,[16] Die Antwoord embodies the ethos of the hip, *Zef*, working class Afrikaner culture. The band members deliberately position themselves as part of a poor white lineage. For example, in the YouTube clip "*Zef* side" (stewartridgway, 2010b), they talk about their supposedly poor origins. Ninja explains that "DJ Hi-Tech lives with his granny, and then I live with my mom and dad down the road and Yolandi's the next door neighbour" (stewartridgway, 2010b). The clip is shot in a poor suburb of Cape Town and in this way the personas they have created align themselves with an underclass. The tattoos which Ninja sport are emblems of coloured[17] prison gangs, and the band position themselves between different races by also identifying themselves with coloured Afrikaans speakers in the Cape Flats.

Hannelie Marx and Candice Milton write that:

> …by explicitly constructing himself as a poor white living on the borders of the Cape Flats—thus indicating a clear distinction between himself and middle class whites—it is possible that Ninja might be promoting a more hybrid, creolised Afrikaans identity where race and class interact. (2011: 738)

Although the origins of the Afrikaner people lie within a hybrid mixture of Europeans, indigenous people, and imported slaves (Steyn, 2004: 148), part of the upliftment of poor white Afrikaners came about precisely in order to maintain "the racial purity of Afrikaners" (Gordon, 1988: 537), since it was at the lower end of the economic spectrum that racial miscegenation was thought most likely to flourish.[18] The members of Die Antwoord situate themselves within the embattled Afrikaans language, as heterodox, poor, and racially impure Afrikaners. Whereas the *Voëlvry* movement aligned itself in opposition to the elite white ruling class, the *Zef* ethos positions itself firmly in solidarity with a lower class, as well as with the disenfranchised class from other races.

Zef Comedy

Besides Die Antwoord, there are also other examples of *Zef* in recent South African comedy. Over the course of the last ten years, *Zef* has emerged, for example, in the music of Jack Parow, as well as in a number of comedy series for theatre and television. One of these is the popular stage show *The Most Amazing Show*, which also went on to become a successful television series.[19] The show features the characters Corné (Louw Venter) and Twakkie (Rob van Vuuren) who were first popularised by regular appearances at the music festival *Oppikoppi*[20], which is also where all of the examples of *Zef* in this chapter first became known, including Die Antwoord. The two characters from *The Most Amazing Show* both sport an essential *snor* (an outsized moustache), and Twakkie is resplendent in a mullet. Each episode features their failure to create an "amazing" show, and reveals their bumbling ineptitude. Yet, despite their perpetual failure, each instalment also conveys their peculiar camaraderie.

Oppikoppi was also where the troupe *Zef Sketse* first tried out their comedy material. They later went on to create a television series called *Kompleks* (2006–2007), which takes place within a security complex—a reference to the many gated communities prevalent in the high crime suburbs of major cities in South Africa. A number of characters in this show are *Zef*, such as the Du Toits who relocated from their caravan park to the elite complex after winning the Lotto. They embody *Zef* in their use of vulgar slang and in their appearance—Mr Du Toit has heavy side-burns and wears a short sleeved safari suit, while Mrs Du Toit—played by a man in drag—appears in garish make-up with a preposterous wig and exaggerated false nails.

The Du Toits are taken to task by Brumilda, a woman from the "aesthetics committee", who hopes to change their behaviour to something more suitably upper-middle class, or else to have them removed from the complex altogether. Despite their vulgarity, however, the viewer sides with them in showing up Brumilda's snobbishness. They repeatedly show up her attempts to reform them. Brumilda is, ultimately, unable to bring them to heel and the viewer is vindicated when the committee is unable to force them to conform. Despite their ridiculous appearances and mannerisms, the audience is still made to feel that the Du Toit's are, in some ways, more genuine than the posh upper class inhabitants of the complex. A certain quality of *Zef* comes to the fore here, the idea that rudeness can be read as resilience.

As already indicated, the title of the series *Kompleks* plays on the idea of a security complex. It also takes a swipe at the psychological complexes relating to new Afrikaner identity. In this sense, *Zef* might be seen as a sort of defiance of the "colonial cringe" which has defined the condition of many post-colonies, formerly viewed as the provincials of the Euro-American metropolis. After white South Africans spent two generations being ostracised from the world and having their culture embargoed by international sanctions, there was a certain feeling of having been rejected by the international community. During apartheid, there was a sense of shame inculcated by the accusations from the international community, and since the end of apartheid there has also been a sense of disgrace in view of a new political dispensation in which aspects of South Africa's history have had to be rewritten. For example, as I had indicated at the start of this chapter, much that was formerly celebrated as part of the Afrikaner heritage has come to be publicly portrayed as disgraceful, and this sense of shame experienced by young Afrikaners has been permitted an outlet in the embrace of the vulgarity embodied by *Zef*. There is something aggressive about *Zef*, about the refusal to conform to the norms prescribed by one's community. This positions its proponents within a tradition of Afrikaner heterodoxy, in that they identify with an ethnic group while challenging its orthodoxies.

Making fun of conditions of poverty and a lack of education may be seen as a brutal joke, but today *Zef* is not only an Afrikaans phenomenon. As can be seen in the opening quotation to this chapter—"I represent South African culture... a lot of different things... blacks, whites, coloureds, English, Afrikaans, Xhosa, Zulu" (stewartridgway, 2010a), *Zef* includes a tacit desire to integrate with other cultures. This may be one approach which those embarrassed by the Afrikaans history of racial segregation have been attempting. Also, some of those performing *Zef* are not from an Afrikaans background, and not necessarily from the lower classes either. A few of the creators of Die Antwoord and *The Most Amazing Show* are products of English private schools and have university educations. In this sense, *Zef* has become more than an Afrikaner phenomenon and has become part of a larger South African context.

There is something idiosyncratic about these performances which make them unique to South Africa. There is also a definite sense of solidarity on the part of the South African audience in being part of the peculiar society which spawned these performances. Fans of *Zef* now include not only Afrikaner whites, but also English whites and Afrikaans coloureds, as well as—since their collaboration with amaXhosa rapper Wanga on "Evil Boy"—an increasing black following.

Internet Identities

I began this chapter by mentioning the *Voëlvry* movement, which gave rise to a number of music festivals around the time of South Africa's historic political transformation. Many of the music festivals which were begun in the early 1990s, such as *Houtstok*, *Rustlers Valley*, *Oppikoppi*, and *Splashy Fen*, are still going strong. There has been an association of *Zef* with festivals from the beginning of its new incarnation as *nouveau chique*, with performers like Jack Parow and comedy shows such as *The Most Amazing Show* and *Zef Sketse*. The *Zef* identity has been closely linked to carnivalesque aspects of the festival experience, such as excess, pleasure, performing youth identities, and experimenting with sexuality. In shifting the arena of the performance of *Zef* to the internet—on sites such as *watkykjy* (what are you looking at)[23], YouTube and Vimeo—a change has occurred in the ways in which the *Zef* ethos contributes to the shaping of identities.

Perhaps the forum, the polis, of South African white youth identity has shifted, or been augmented by the possibilities presented by interacting with others over the internet. There is certainly a difference between being part of the mass participation of a music festival, part of a throng of bodies experiencing the same searing volume, and watching a clip on one's own—in the isolation of one's home. These *fora* manufacture very different types of identity creation and substantiation. Watching Die Antwoord on YouTube and Vimeo personalises the festivalisation of one's own private space. It is a more fragmented and reflective experience, no longer part of a present sharing of the public space, and it potentially permits a more analytical response.

Yet, the community created by internet clips is often premised on personal connections. For example, I first saw an Antwoord clip when a friend living in China forwarded it to me. In this way, an internet community is set up by links which continuously shape a living culture between individual connections. Also, over the internet, interactions with strangers tend to be more extreme, since they are largely anonymous. There is something transitory about making a comment to a passing stranger at a festival, whereas an ill-considered remark on an internet comments page is likely to remain there for a very long time to come. These remarks are often more personal and outspoken, because they occur from within the privacy of one's own home, and yet they can also be more flippant and irresponsible, since one may not necessarily be identified as the originator of a comment, or face the consequences of a backlash against it.

Also, social media like YouTube offers South Africans the opportunity of becoming aware of how the *Zef* phenomenon has been received by outsiders. It can be argued that one's conceptions of national identity coalesce when placed in contrast to other cultures. What has hitherto been invisible becomes pronounced. In other words, signifiers which had become almost unconscious—accents, colloquialisms, cultural references —become identifiable as different. Once these have been removed from their surrounding contexts, they are able to become objects of curiosity, available for scrutiny. In this sense, by participating in internet message-boards, one is able to reflect on one's national identity and one's location within it without ever leaving home.

Reading through the comments which people have made on sites featuring clips by, or about, Die Antwoord, one finds an on-going debate about authenticity, and whether Die Antwoord are "real" or not. Where some people have doubted their veracity, others have defended Jones' role as Ninja. They have cited, for example, the onstage personas adopted by

David Bowie, Marilyn Manson, Madonna, Gene Simmons, and Stefani Germanotta's creation of Lady Gaga.[24] These are apt comparisons, which make a strong case for the deliberate artifice an artist is able to adopt, and yet, interestingly enough, none of the cases cited have ever managed to relinquish or transcend their national identities. For instance, even in his golden Ziggy Stardust cat suit, David Bowie remains identifiably British. Similarly, Madonna may have referenced Marilyn Monroe, Blondie, and any number of iconic figures by means of her ever-changing personas, yet all of her incarnations remain recognisably American. I wonder why it seems so difficult to disguise one's national identity. In an interview promoting the performance of his work at the Sonar festival in Barcelona, Steve Reich said:

> I think all music comes from a time and a place... the composers that we know and love give honest expression to [this locatedness]... you just are who you are, and... [your] music will bear evidence to the honesty of your situation, no matter what it is... (Sonar, 2011)

There is something idiosyncratic about Die Antwoord's personas. Even though they play with multiple identities and parody any number of ethnicities, something about them gives them away as uniquely South African. Certainly, there is a sense of solidarity on the part of an audience in feeling part of the peculiar society that spawned the band. For example, with comments such as:

> lol guys u wont get this if your not South African... Its brilliant (crow99100)

> This is South African Awesome (mataworks)[25]

There are also others embarrassed by the uncouth vulgarity of Die Antwoord, but in their discomfort they nevertheless identify themselves as South African, and the band as part of the local landscape. In a sense, Ninja might be seen as a personification of his location—as parody, as pastiche, as make-believe—because South Africa is a made up country, fabricated by a global community as well as by ever-changing perspectives of its heterogeneous history. South Africa was invented as much by the Dutch East India Company and the British Commonwealth, as it has been by the African National Congress (ANC). In a way, this is not altogether different from the way that Jones has created and sustained his identity as Ninja by piecing together the bric-a-brac forms of contesting discourses. For all its posturing, *Zef* might be seen as an authentic representation—albeit exaggerated—of a confused, multi-lingual, emerging national identity. This identity has been disseminated in popular music, television, magazines, stage shows, and now also, most powerfully, by the internet.[26]

Conclusion

Within *Zef's* mockery of the poor white Afrikaner resides an attempt to come to terms with some of the unsettling qualities inherent in a new South African white identity. This is an identity which has had to reshape itself within the context of a hybrid culture. I would like to end this chapter with a final reflection on the essay by Christopher Ballantine, referred to earlier. Ballantine quotes Njabulo Ndebele who claims that "whiteness" had to:

> undergo an experiential transformation by absorbing new cultural experiences as an essential condition for achieving a new sense of cultural rootedness. (2004: 106)

In order to maintain their sense of belonging, white Afrikaners could no longer resort to an identity forged in opposition to the British Empire, or even (as was the case during apartheid) against the anti-apartheid movements in the democracies of the West and the "Communist" East. Facing the ignominy of the poor white identity and revelling in it, exaggerating it, and parodying it[27] have all been attempts at transformation, since it was the elite white Afrikaners who had been responsible for the iniquities of the past. These have been moves against the authority of the former Afrikaner hegemony. As Vestergaard again writes:

> Whereas the Afrikaner establishment during Apartheid promoted an authoritarian collective identity, the Afrikaner artists are exploring an explicitly anti-authoritarian identity with fluid boundaries, open to all kinds of global as well as local African influences. (2011: 35)

Identification with *Zef* has permitted an outlet for an amorphous, ambiguous ethos which refuses to be tied down to conventional morays. Robert Gordon writes that apartheid was "rooted in the idea that the Afrikaners' identity should be protected" (1988: 549). It follows then that being anti-apartheid would imply a diffusion—if not an outright destruction—of that identity. One of the ways to challenge this identity has been to embrace everything the Afrikaner identity had been protected from in the past, including poverty and the "impurity" of other races.

Amanda du Preez points out that, "the impurity of Zef appears to be invoked as an exalted hybridity" (2011: 107) which challenges notions of ethnic unity.

Die Antwoord are simultaneously self-denying and self-promoting—they are self-denigrating and arrogant, appealing to both an artificial showmanship and authenticity. In contrast to Ninja and Yo-landi's attitude as poseurs, the Afrikaans *Voëlvry* revolution of 1989 maintained a very definite identity as an authentic counter-culture. It was a movement for social change, which opposed the dogma of a political party (the National Party) and the entrenched, state sanctioned Calvinistic religion (the *Nederduitse Gereformeerde Kerk*) on which it had been premised.[28] But in Die Antwoord, *Kompleks*, and *The Most Amazing Show*, one gets the feeling that they are not only mocking the establishment by sneering at it from a *Zef* perspective, but also parodying the idea of being *Zef*. It almost feels like parody for its own sake—an exuberant irreverence and a flamboyant display without any fixed enemy or goal.

These performers do not appear to be in opposition to any particular power system, except perhaps the politics of good taste. As Marx and Milton put it:

> They have opened up a space for a generation increasingly fed up with politics and the burden of being white and Afrikaans in post-Apartheid South Africa. (2011: 743)

Whereas the counter-culture of the late apartheid era tried to provide a solution to the problems of the day, Die Antwoord, (which means "The Answer"), do not provide any answers at all.[29] In one of their initial promotional clips, Ninja is asked what they provide the answer to and he replies with a casual, throwaway line: "Fuck, whatever man" (stewartridgway, 2010b). In this line reside an apathetic lacklustre disposition towards fixed meanings, a lack of concern for established truths, and a disdain for solutions. There is both an air of resignation, of giving over to whatever meaning might be supplied by others, as well as an attitude of irreconcilable defiance.

Notes

1. An earlier draft of this chapter was presented as a paper at Performance Studies International #16 (Camillo 2), an international conference held in Utrecht, the Netherlands, from 25—29 May 2011. Extracts from it also formed part of a round table discussion published in a special issue of *SAFUNDI* (*The Journal of South African and American Studies*) in 2012.
2. Afrikaans for "whatever".
3. From the introduction to "Enter the Ninja", YouTube (stewartridgway, 2010a). [Online] Available at: <www.youtube.com/watch?v=wc3f4xU_FfQ> (Accessed 12 May 2011).
4. Archbishop Desmond Tutu is generally credited with having first described South Africa as a "Rainbow Nation".
5. News24, 2011. Interview with Die Antwoord. [online video] Available at: <http://www.news24.com/Multimedia/Entertainment/Interview-with-Die-Antwoord-20110916> (Accessed 16 December 2011).
6. Zef not only denotes the term "vulgar" in the usual sense of the word, but also with a nod to its origin in the Latin vulgaris for "mob" or "commoners".
7. The South African Border War refers to the conflict between South Africa and South West Africa (later renamed Namibia, after independence) and Angola, from 1966–1989.
8. The Voortrekkers (literally "forward pullers") were the pioneering Afrikaners who left the Cape Colony in the 1830s to escape British rule.
9. The name means "free as a bird" and also has connotations to being an "outlaw".
10. See Hannelie Marx and Viola Candice Milton (2011: 735).
11. Melissa Steyn notes that the:

> early settlers of mixed European, though primarily Dutch, ancestry unified in a common identification as Afrikaners, people of Africa, and retained little actual or sentimental attachment to their European homelands. (2004: 148)

12. The exclusive ethnic definition of an Afrikaner "volk", reinforced by the Nationalist apartheid government, has become problematised in the New South Africa by attempts to extend the categorisation of "Afrikaners" to include all speakers of the Afrikaans language (an indigenous creolised version of Dutch), which include many coloured (or "Brown") people.
13. The Nederduits-Gereformeerde Kerk originated in South Africa from the Dutch Reformed Church in the seventeenth century, a Protestant Church founded on the teachings of John Calvin.
14. Robert Gordon (1988: 537), summarises research undertaken by Adam and Giliomee (1979:150), about the formation of the Nationalist government in 1948:

The issue that dominated Afrikaner intellectual life was that of the (largely Afrikaner) poor whites. A series of factors ranging from ecological catastrophes, the ravages of the Anglo-Boer War and the Depression had served to push the number of poor, if not destitute, whites up from 106 000 in 1921 to 300 000 in 1933

15. Caravan parks are the South African equivalent of American trailer parks.
16. Afrikaans: fuck, pussy, fuck, cunt.
17. In South Africa, the expression "coloured" is used to designate somebody of mixed race. It is not considered an offensive term (as it is in the United States) and is employed as a term of self-definition.
18. Saul Dubow notes that for Geoff Cronje, a Pretoria University professor of sociology who helped to disseminate apartheid as a sociological necessity, the notion "that poorer whites are particularly vulnerable to racial intermixture remain[ed] a constant focus of anxiety" (1992: 239).
19. First produced in 2000 as a series of stage productions—written, directed, produced, and starring Rob van Vuuren and Louw Venter—TMAS (*The Most Amazing Show*) went on to have three successful seasons on the television channel SABC 2 (2006–2007). At the time of writing, the two characters created by the series continue to be employed as hosts for events—such as the popular rock festival, *Oppikoppi*—as well as appearing regularly on television and radio.
20. *Oppikoppi* is the most successful popular music festival in South Africa. First started in 1994 on a farm near the mining town of Northam, it is today a multi-genre festival attracting approximately 15,000 spectators annually.
21. It should be noted that not all Afrikaners endorse the hybrid vulgarity of Zef, and more traditional Afrikaners have scorned the emergence of Zef as belittling of the Afrikaner heritage and a betrayal of its values.
22. See comments on the web pages by: Gittins, 2010; Gabe, 2010; and Reddit, 2011.
23. From the comments page of "Enter the Ninja" on YouTube (stewartridgway, 2010a).
24. It seems ironic that the medium that formerly defined the mass media (television) has in this instance been the most limiting form. It is highly unlikely that anybody outside of South Africa has so much as heard of the Zef television series *Kompleks*. However, after building up a following over a decade, the stage show *The Most Amazing Show* and Zef musician Jack Parow have performed in Europe, and Die Antwoord are currently embarking on their second world tour.
25. As Brendan Jury says:

> parody and pastiche give the alternative musicians [in South Africa] a vehicle for adopting new resistant identities in a re-negotiation of self-definition. (1996: 102)

26. The Christian denomination was famously parodied in the naming of Johannes Kerkorrel's "Gereformeerde Blues Band".
27. In contrast to the explicit political ideological stance of… the alternative movements that went before [Die Antwoord] are not overtly political and do not attempt to make openly ideological statements… there is an almost banal, nihilist notion, denying boundaries and celebrating a hybrid identity that resists being named - or compartmentalised. (Marx and Milton, 2011: 734)

References

Adam, H. and Giliomee, H. (1979) *The Rise and Crisis of Afrikaner Power.* Cape Town: David Philip.

Ballantine, C. (2004) "Re-thinking 'Whiteness'? Identity, Change and 'White' Popular Music in Post-Apartheid South Africa." *Popular Music* 23(2): pp. 105–131.

Delahaye, G. (2010) "Die Antwoord Is 'Fake', And So What?" *Videogum* (3 February). [online]. Available at: <http://videogum.com/112671/die_antwoord_is_fake_and_so_wh/back lashes/> (Accessed 16 December 2011).

Dubow, S. (1992) "Afrikaner Nationalism, Apartheid and the Conceptualization of 'Race'." *The Journal of African History* 33(2): pp. 209–237.

Du Preez, A. (2011) "Die Antwoord Gooi *Zef* Liminality: Of Monsters, Carnivals and Affects." *Image & Text* 35(17). [online] Available at: <http://www.imageandtext.up.ac.za/index.php/issues/35-number-17-2011> (Accessed 7 June 2012).

Gittins, I. (2010) "Die Antwoord—Review." *The Guardian* (16 November). [online]. Available at: <http://www.guardian.co.uk/music/2010/nov/16/die-antwoord-review> (Accessed 16 December 2011).

Gordon, R. (1988) "Apartheid's Anthropologists: The Genealogy of Afrikaner Anthropology." *American Ethnologist* 15(3): pp. 535–553.

Harrison, D. (1986) *The White Tribe of Africa.* Johannesburg: Macmillan.

Jury, B. (1996) "Boys to Men: Afrikaans Alternative Popular Music 1986–1990." *African Languages and Cultures* 9(2), Special Issue: Gender and Popular Culture: pp. 99–109.

Kompleks, (2006–2007) [television series] Pit Productions. SABC 2.

Marx, H. and Milton, V. C. (2011) "Bastardised Whiteness: 'Zef'-culture, Die Antwoord and the Reconfiguration of Contemporary Afrikaans identities." *Social Identities* 17(6): pp. 723–745.

News24. (2011) *Interview with Die Antwoord.* [online video] Available at: <http://www.news24.com/Multimedia/Entertainment/Interview-with-Die-Antwoord-20110916> (Accessed 16 December 2011).

Reddit. (2011) "Die Antwoord's Ninja at Occupy Wall Street." [online] Available at: <http://www.reddit.com/r/Music/comments/l8vnz/die_antwoords_ninja_at_occupy_wall_street/> (Accessed 16 December 2011).

Reuters. (2010) "Growing Number of Poor White South Africans." *Business Report* (26 March). [online]. Available at: <http://www.iol.co.za/business/business-news/growing-number-of-poor-whites-south-african-1.813776> (Accessed 24 September 2010).

SABC 3—Top Billing. (2010) *Jeannie D Braai's with Die Antwoord.* [online] Available at: http://www.topbilling.com/articles/Jeannie-D-Braais-With-Die-Antwoord.html?articleID=716> (Accessed 16 December 2011).

The Most Amazing Show, (2006-2007) [television series] Pandamonium Productions. SABC 2.

Sonar. (2011) "Concerts and DJ's 2011—Steve Reich: Music for 18 Musicians." *Promotional page of the 18th International Festival of Advanced Music and New Media Art of Barcelona.* [online video] Available at: <http://2011.sonar.es/en/artistes/steve-reich-bcn216-synergy-vocals_306.html> (Accessed 16 December 2011).

stewartridgway. (2010a) *Die Antwoord – Enter The Ninja (Official)* [online video] Available at: <http://www.YouTube.com/watch?v=wc3f4xU_FfQ> (Accessed 15 September 2010).

stewartridgway. (2010b) *Die Antwoord—Zef Side (Official)* [online video] Available at: <http://www.YouTube.com/watch?v=Q77YBmtd2Rw&feature=player_embedded> (Accessed 16 December 2011).

Steyn, M. E. (2004) "Rehabilitating a Whiteness Disgraced: Afrikaner *White Talk* in Post-Apartheid South Africa." *Communication Quarterly* 52(2) Spring. pp. 143–169.

Vestergaard, M. (2001) "Who's Got the Map?: The Negotiation of Afrikaner Identities in Post-Apartheid South Africa." *Daedalus* 130(1) Winter. Special Issue: Why South Africa Matters: pp. 19–44.

CONTRIBUTORS

Gowon Ama Doki holds a PhD in Theatre Arts with a bias in Theatre Semiotics from the University of Abuja, Nigeria. He is currently Associate Professor and Head of the Department of Theatre Arts at the Benue State University, Makurdi, Nigeria. His main research interests include indigenous theatre studies, semiotics, and development communication, as well as literary theory and criticism. His book, *Traditional Theatre in Perspective: Signs and Signification in Igbe, Igirinya and Kwagh-hir*, remains a major contribution to literature on indigenous theatre in Nigeria. He has been Editor of the *Makurdi Journal of Arts and Culture (MAJAC)* since 2006.

Patrick Ebewo is professor and head of the Department of Drama and Film, Tshwane University of Technology, South Africa. He has taught at universities in Nigeria, Lesotho, Swaziland, and Botswana. He is a Rated Researcher, who has published extensively in the areas of African drama, applied theatre, culture, and film studies. He has won many research awards and is a member of many professional bodies, including the International Federation for Theatre Research (IFTR) and African Theatre Association (AfTA).

Johan Esterhuizen (Johannes Theuins Esterhuizen) obtained a B.Dram degree from Stellenbosch University in 1969 and joined the Cape Performing Arts Board (CAPAB) Drama Company in the following year. He also holds an M.Dram degree with specialist fields of interest in Interactive and Applied Theatre. Esterhuizen left for London in 1971 and taught at Forest School near Snaresbrook, before returning to South Africa. Esterhuizen re-joined CAPAB in 1977 and was appointed Head of Drama in 1986. He later joined the staff of the University of Stellenbosch Drama Department in 1990. Esterhuizen has travelled extensively to other African countries, including a teaching stint at Moi University, Kenya. He retired from Stellenbosch University at the end of 2012 and is now focused on community theatre and his work as a theatre and film practitioner.

Dr **Kene Igweonu** is Assistant Head of the Department of Music and Performing Arts at Canterbury Christ Church University, UK. He is a member of the editorial boards of *African Performance Review* and *South African Theatre Journal*. Dr Igweonu is founding convener, and currently co-convener of the African and Caribbean Theatre and Performance Working Group of the International Federation for Theatre Research. His research and practice interests are in somatic practices in performance training, issues of identity in performance, and cross-art practices. In addition to publications in peer-reviewed journals, he has written several entries on Nigerian theatre for the *Cambridge Encyclopaedia of Stage Actors and Acting*, and edited *Trends in Twenty-First Century African Theatre and Performance*—published in 2011 by Rodopi.

Ofonime Inyang is a doctoral candidate in drama and film at the Tshwane University of Technology, Pretoria, South Africa. His research draws on applied theatre principles for development communication, targeting environmental problems in rural communities in Sub-Saharan Africa. He is a Nigerian dramatist, poet, journalist, and university teacher. He teaches applied theatre, directing, alternative media courses and writes plays and proposals for organisations in Nigeria and South Africa. His works appear in local and international outlets, including *International Literary Quarterly*. He has attended conferences, presented papers, and contributed chapters to books in a wide range of fields, and recently bagged the Graduate Scholar Award (2012) in Montreal, Canada, for significant scholastic achievement and leadership skills.

Anton Krueger teaches performance studies and creative writing at Rhodes University, South Africa. His research interests include questions around identity in contemporary South Africa. He has published numerous reviews, articles, and book chapters on post-apartheid theatre, as well as the book: *Experiments in Freedom: Issues of Identity in New South African Drama* (2010). Krueger has also published creative writing in a range of genres, including *Sunnyside Sal* (novella, 2010), *Shaggy* (comedy monologues, written with Pravasan Pillay, 2011), *and Everyday Anomalies* (poetry, 2011). His plays have been performed in eight countries and have been nominated for a number of national and international awards, including the VITA and the Olive Schreiner.

Karabelo Lekalake holds an MA degree in Drama and Theatre Arts, and is a junior lecturer at the University of the Free State, South Africa. Her directorial debut was at the 2007 Zwakala Arts Festival with the play *The*

Dead Politician. She has since directed a number of student productions at the Drama Department, University of the Free State. In 2011, Lekalake directed *Plastics*, produced by Performing Arts Council of the Free State (PACOFS). She has since then produced and directed *Chasing Laughter* (2012) which was funded by the National Arts Council of South Africa.

Janine Lewis currently lectures at the Tshwane University of Technology Department of Drama and Film, South Africa. Lewis holds a doctoral degree focusing on devising, montage, and contemporary performance. She has taught masterclasses and presented various papers in Greece, Chile, Prague, Wales, Netherlands, America, Canada and South Africa. She has successfully published in a number of reputable journals as well as contributing chapters in books. Lewis is also a performance artist creating site-specific solo and collaborative pieces with a variety of performers, fine artists, and digital artists—*www.seity.co.za*.

Christopher Joseph Odhiambo is Professor of Literature and Applied Drama at Moi University's Department of Literature, Theatre and Film Studies. He has presented papers in numerous workshops, seminars, conferences and symposia locally and internationally. Professor Odhiambo is widely published in reputable journals and books on literature, theatre, film and radio.

Christine Odi (PhD) gained her postgraduate degrees from the University of Ibadan, Ibadan, Nigeria. She is currently teaching at the Department of Fine, Industrial and Theatre Arts, Faculty of Arts, Niger Delta University, Bayelsa State, Nigeria. She teaches theatre history, dramatic literature, costume and make-up arts, research methods, and community theatre for development. In addition to her taught courses, her other areas of interest include: studies in advanced arts and culture, women empowerment studies and Niger Delta drama and theatre.

Professor **Osita Okagbue** holds a BA, MA, MA and PhD in Drama and Theatre from the University of Nigeria at Nsukka, the University of Ibadan, Nigeria and the University of Leeds respectively. He is the founding President of the African Theatre Association (AfTA) and founding/current Editor of *African Performance Review* (*APR*). He is also an Associate Editor for Routledge's *Theatres of the World Series*. His published works include *African Theatres and Performances* (Routledge 2007), *Culture and Identity in African and Caribbean Theatre* (Adonis and Abbey, 2009), and *African Theatre: Diasporas* (James Currey) co-edited with Christine Matzke. Professor Okagbue serves on the Board of Governors of Collective Artists, a South East London-based community theatre company support by the Arts Council of England.

Dr **Victor Ukaegbu** is Associate Professor of Theatre and Performance, University of Northampton. He has published in the areas of African, Black British and African diaspora theatres, in applied theatre and ethnodrama, in intercultural and postcolonial performances. He is the author of *The Use of Masks in Igbo Theatre in Nigeria: the Aesthetic Flexibility of Performance Traditions* (2007), founding member of African Theatre Association (AfTA), co-artistic director of Jawi Theatre Collective, and associate Editor, *African Performance Review*. He is on the editorial board of *Journal of Applied Arts and Health* and is contributing researcher on World Scenography.

INDEX